CHERISHED GIFTS

DEVOTIONS FOR MOMS BY A MOM

KATIE MARTIN

NORTHWESTERN PUBLISHING HOUSE
Milwaukee, Wisconsin

Cover photo: Shutterstock
Art Director: Karen Knutson
Designer: Sarah Messner

Northwestern Publishing House
1250 N. 113th St., Milwaukee, WI 53226-3284
www.nph.net
© 2015 Northwestern Publishing House
Published 2015
Printed in the United States of America
ISBN 978-0-8100-2669-8
ISBN 978-0-8100-2670-4 (e-book)

With love and thanks

> *to my parents for a lifetime of support.*
> *to my children for providing humor and a reason to write.*
> *to my husband for his encouragement and patience.*

CONTENTS

Cherished Gifts was written by a mom for moms. Katie Martin knows the challenges, frustrations, and joys you experience each day as a mother. Katie cherishes the spiritual guidance in God's Word that her parents gave her, and she continues to pass on that guidance to her children. Knowing that God's Word has comforted her during struggles as a parent, she hopes to encourage you with God's Word as you carry out your job as a mother.

A picture of a gift is next to the opening message and also next to three devotions interspersed within this book. When you come to each of these pictures, take a breath, pause, and think about the gifts of God, including the gift of children. Katie knows that especially on tough days, moms need to do that!

The first message is Katie's letter *to you* and her hopes *for you.*

Lynn A. Groth
Editor

A CHERISHED GIFT

The package came wrapped in plain brown paper and encased in layers of thick tape. Dirt and debris clung to the sticky residue where the packing tape had begun to peel away. Although the exterior of the package was tattered and unsightly, inside was the most beautiful gift—a necklace of alternating pearls and crystal beads carefully restrung from my grandmother's jewelry. The crystal beads trapped the sunlight and then let it loose again in tiny pinpricks of dazzling light. The necklace may have looked extremely valuable in my hand, but its true worth could never be converted to dollars and cents. The box arrived only weeks after my grandmother went home to heaven. The necklace is a physical remembrance of her, and it is an heirloom that I can pass on to my daughter. It is a gift to cherish.

From the first moment we hold our newborn children, we realize the magnitude of the blessings we have received. A tiny baby is a beautiful gift from a loving God. But even though precious newborns seem innocent, they come to us in tattered packages. Growing children pitch full-fledged temper tantrums and defy us at every turn. Through sleep-deprived eyes, we see that our children are exactly like us—sinners in need of a Savior.

Even though the Holy Spirit works faith in their tiny hearts through Baptism, a staggering responsibility still remains for us. Our charge as Christian mothers is to tell these little ones about the great love of Jesus and that he died on a cross to earn heaven for them. And this task has an impending deadline. These children are not ours to keep but, rather, are on loan from God to train and prepare to go back to him. Children are one of the few blessings that can go to heaven with us.

Caring for children can seem like an insurmountable challenge, but we find comfort in knowing that motherhood is not a solo journey. The support of a spouse, family, and friends is great, but far more important is the support of our loving and almighty God. As we walk the path of motherhood, he is beside us through triumphs and sorrows alike.

He tends his flock like a shepherd: He gathers the lambs in his arms and carries them close to his heart; he gently leads those that have young. (Isaiah 40:11)

These beautiful words of Isaiah remind us that God holds our children close to his heart. But his loving care extends beyond our children. He also leads the ones who have the young, namely, mothers. Our Good Shepherd cares for us as well!

It is my prayer that this book and the Scriptures within it strengthen you and me in our role as Christian mothers. As we grow in our faith and delight in the peace that Jesus brings, let's pass the pearls of this peace on to our children. On days that threaten our sanity and challenge our senses, we can be assured that our loving Shepherd stands by our side with his guidance and love. On those few and far between days on which all things go well, let's praise the One responsible.

Through the grit of hardship, the monotony of daily tasks, and both the smooth and bumpy roads of life, God gives us joy beyond measure. He gives us children. Let's cherish each moment with them, remembering that our God helps us bear the responsibility of leading our little lambs to him.

Your sister in Christ,

Katie Martin

DON'T BE ANXIOUS ABOUT ANYTHING?!

Rejoice in the Lord always. I will say it again: Rejoice! Let your gentleness be evident to all. The Lord is near. Do not be anxious about anything, but in every situation, by prayer and petition, with thanksgiving, present your requests to God. And the peace of God, which transcends all understanding, will guard your hearts and your minds in Christ Jesus. (Philippians 4:4-7)

Find your happy place is a phrase used by some mental health professionals. They say that finding one's happy place will help combat stress and foster positive emotional well-being. Some magazine articles and online blogs promote the idea that having a happy place can release tension and separate an individual from the pressures of day-to-day living.

What is your happy place? A nap in a hammock near the beach or a hike to a craggy summit may provide a temporary happy place. But even in relaxing places, worry soon roots itself in our hearts. We stress about kids, confrontations with coworkers, or never-ending to-do lists.

We can try to escape trials in pursuit of a happy place, but Satan is there too. He drives the spike of anxiety between joy in Christ and us. Walls of worry surround us, keeping us from putting complete confidence in the rock-solid promises of God. Even while reading the words of comfort Paul wrote to the Philippians, the voice of sinfulness persists in our minds.

Do not be anxious about anything. (Philippians 4:6)

Don't be anxious about anything? You've got to be kidding! My child's fever is almost off the charts, and I'm not supposed to worry?

Paul knew anxiety. As he wrote his letter to the Philippians, he was under house arrest, awaiting trial before the Roman government. He was restricted in his preaching. However, Paul knew that his true source of joy was not found in his earthly circumstances, but in Christ. He urged the Philippians to rejoice in the Lord *always.*

How does a Christian rejoice even in the face of devastating circumstances? Like Paul, we know that the true source of joy comes only through Christ Jesus. We have the knowledge that Christ has completed our salvation and has promised to be with us through thick and thin. This enables true joy to spill over and to shine light on even the darkest moments.

We cannot escape the temporary troubles we face on earth. Fortunately, neither can we escape the all-encompassing, never-ending love of our Savior. The arms of our loving Savior are wrapped around us and allow us to look forward to our true happy place—heaven. The next time you and I feel a surge of anxiety about to crash over us, let's take a deep breath and retreat to this happy place. Let's imagine standing in heaven with the angels praising Jesus for all eternity with no more crying, pain, or worry. Now that's a reason to rejoice! That's a most happy place!

Dear Lord, be with me today and help me to rejoice in all circumstances, praising your name in both good times and bad. Take away my anxiety, and deliver me from the worries that plague my mind. Reassure me of the peace that surpasses all understanding that I possess through Jesus. I pray in his name. Amen.

Strength from God's Word: Read I Peter 1:8,9. What is the source of our inexpressible joy? Read I Peter 4:12-19. Why can Christians rejoice even in the face of persecution?

FEARLESS EVANGELIST

In your hearts revere Christ as Lord. Always be prepared to give an answer to everyone who asks you to give the reason for the hope that you have. But do this with gentleness and respect. (1 Peter 3:15)

A shopping emergency had arisen. I needed a new dress for a family wedding, and time was running out. After ravaging the sale racks, I raced to a fitting room. With two toddlers in tow, this would not be an ideal shopping experience. But desperation had set in.

Because my son's attention span is less than five seconds, he soon tired of being my fashion advisor. Driven by curiosity, he ducked under the fitting room wall, peered into the next stall, and belted out a loud rendition of "The Bible is God's Word." Although his serenade earned chuckles from the kind ladies in the fitting room, I apologized, red-faced, and scooted both kids to the checkout.

Sandwiched between the humor and embarrassment of the situation was a lesson in evangelism. My son didn't choose to sing "The Wheels on the Bus" or "Itsy-Bitsy Spider." Instead, he sang about the value of the Word of God. He did this without fear of ridicule or embarrassment.

Children are amazing evangelists. We hear their simple, heartfelt confessions in Sunday school and in their prayers at night. Children are proud of the salvation Jesus earned for them and accept God's Word at face value instead of questioning every facet of it. Jesus praised childlike faith:

> *Truly I tell you, unless you change and become like little children, you will never enter the kingdom of heaven. Therefore, whoever takes the lowly position of this child is the greatest in the kingdom of heaven. (Matthew 18:3,4)*

Perhaps it is our fear of embarrassment that hinders us from sharing our faith with childlike enthusiasm. We adults have a keen realization that others might make fun of us or reject our message. Our concerns are based on our desire for worldly acceptance and popularity. Like Moses at the burning bush, our excuses continue to pour out: "Not today, God." "I'm not a good speaker." "I'm just not sure what to say." "I don't want to lose her as a friend."

But our God is amazing. He uses fumbling humans steeped in sinfulness to proclaim his powerful message. God used stammering Moses to speak forcefully to Pharaoh. He changed Peter from one who denied his Savior into a bold sharer of the hope that he had through Christ.

Instead of focusing on our own inadequacies, we can focus on the power of the message and the peace it brings into the lives of those who hear and believe it. Souls will die without the knowledge of a loving Savior who took their sins to the cross. Every day we can be evangelists. We can pray for pastors, teachers, and missionaries around the world and contribute to the work they carry out. We can share peace through Christ daily with our children through family devotions. We can ask that God use our words and actions as lights to bring others to learn about him.

Pray that we will always be prepared to give a reason for the hope we have. Although the location most likely will not be under a fitting room stall, may we share the joy of Jesus wherever and whenever the opportunity arises!

———————

Dear Lord, today I pray for pastors, teachers, and missionaries who proclaim the gospel throughout the world. Bless their efforts and send the Holy Spirit to bring many to faith through the message they preach. Help me be an evangelist in my own life as well. Take away any fear or hesitation as I share your Word in my home, with my friends, and with whomever you put in my path. In Jesus' name. Amen.

Strength from God's Word: Read Hebrews 4:12. How do these words encourage us as evangelists? Read 2 Corinthians 4:5-7. How do these words remind us that evangelism isn't about us and what we can do?

MISSING THE POINT

What good will it be for someone to gain the whole world, yet forfeit their soul? Or what can anyone give in exchange for their soul? (Matthew 16:26)

The scene was reminiscent of an Easter greeting card. The cross on a church had become a silhouette against a backdrop of thunderhead clouds shaded orange and purple by the setting sun. Bending low, I attempted to direct my children to gaze at the beautiful sunset. Although their heads were turned in the right direction, their eyes weren't focused on the sunset. My son exclaimed, "Yeah, the light is beautiful!" Standing there like a deer frozen by headlights, he completely missed the point. His eyes were so entranced by the bright spotlight in front of the cross that he failed to see anything beyond it.

We mothers know that children frequently miss the point. Punishment doesn't always prevent them from repeating the same infraction as soon as one's back is turned. An entire book can be lost to a single detail or picture that they find interesting. Yet how often do we adult children of God miss the point? Often we are like deer in the headlights, so focused on our earthly concerns that we fail to see the beauty of God's promises directly in front of us.

When the concerns of this world bog us down and cause us to lose focus on God's promises, he is there to redirect us with his Word. Think of Mary and Martha (Luke 10:38-42). Mary and Martha were blessed by a home visit from the King of kings and Lord of lords! While Mary stayed focused, listening intently to the words of Jesus, Martha began to fret about the details. She was a whirlwind of activity, preparing her house for the Savior. Who could blame her? As Martha scurried around baking the bread, cooking the meal, and sweeping the dusty floor for her special guest, she became angry as her sister sat and seemingly did nothing.

Jesus patiently redirected Martha, gently taking her focus away from earthly details and back to heavenly matters:

The Lord answered her, "Martha, Martha, you are anxious and troubled about many things, but one thing is necessary." (Luke 10:41,42 ESV)

How often aren't we like Martha? We scurry madly from here to there, attempting to conquer the never-ending list of daily tasks and focusing so much energy on them that we forfeit spiritual time in the process. How often hasn't the busyness of daily life pushed a family devotion out of first place on your agenda or mine? How often aren't we too tired at night to finish the prayers we finally got around to starting?

Through his Word, Jesus does the same thing for us that he did for Martha long ago. He redirects us with his words and puts our focus back where it belongs—on his cross. At the cross we find full forgiveness for all our distracted moments and for all the times we have pushed Christ out of first place. At the cross we stand refreshed and renewed, ready to serve our crucified, resurrected Lord and equipped with the knowledge that only one thing is needful.

> One thing's needful; Lord, this treasure
> Teach me highly to regard.
> All else, though it first give pleasure,
> Is a yoke that presses hard.
> Beneath it the heart is still fretting and striving,
> No true, lasting happiness ever deriving.
> This one thing is needful; all others are vain—
> I count all but loss that I Christ may obtain.
> (*Christian Worship* hymn 290)

The things we chase after here in this world will one day suffer the same fate as the world itself. They are fleeting and temporary, but the Word of God and the salvation it works last for eternity.

Dear Jesus, focus my eyes of faith back on you instead of on the flurry of activity in my life. Each day of my walk through this earthly life, keep my eyes focused on your cross. In your name, I pray. Amen.

Strength from God's Word: Read Philippians 3:7,8. What was of utmost importance to Paul? What did he consider all earthly matters to be? What are some ways you can focus more on growing in God's grace each day?

MUST BE NICE

Keep your lives free from the love of money and be content with what you have, because God has said, "Never will I leave you; never will I forsake you." (Hebrews 13:5)

"Must be nice" has become my mantra of discontent. I repeat this motto whenever someone else's life looks more appealing than my own. When my sister *has* to go shopping so that her housekeeper can clean, I grumble about the never-ending tornado of dirt in my own house and mutter, "Must be nice." As a friend flips through photos of her exotic vacation, I smile but think, "Must be nice." The only exotic place I visit is the jungle of my overgrown backyard that has been overtaken by hostile fire ants!

As the world charms us with material wealth, the devil daily tempts us to grumble about our lives. We yearn for more money, better vehicles, longer vacations, less stressful jobs, or bigger houses. Television ads and mail order catalogs bombard us with all the must-haves. Luxuries beyond our wildest dreams promise to make us happy, but instead they empty our checking accounts and fill us with a desire for more. Paul described this very trap:

The love of money is a root of all kinds of evil. Some people, eager for money, have wandered from the faith and pierced themselves with many griefs. (1 Timothy 6:10)

With materialism and discontent in the driver's seat, we put God and his spiritual riches in the backseat. Our Savior, who was tempted in every way as we are but who never sinned, understood the lure of this materialistic world. In his Sermon on the Mount, Jesus set our priorities straight:

Seek first the kingdom of God and his righteousness, and all these things will be added to you. (Matthew 6:33 ESV)

What does it mean to seek God's kingdom first? It means that Jesus is our number one, lifelong priority. We seek ways every day to know him in his Word, to grow in his grace, and to share him with others. And when we set our sights on the Lord first, the floodgates of heavenly blessings open on us. No, this doesn't mean we will be awarded the lottery jackpot or be given accolades because of our earthly successes. Rather, when Christ has the number one place in our lives, we are promised blessings beyond measure from a God who has promised to work all things out for good. Our God, who gave his own Son to solve our biggest problem of sin, will certainly take care of all the other details of life.

Chasing after the material things of this world offers us no lasting peace or contentment. True peace comes from knowing Christ and that we are at peace with God because of Christ's saving work. True contentment comes from knowing that our God is vigilantly watching over us and providing for us each and every moment.

Hebrews 13:5 says it beautifully. God will *never* leave us. Can any of our earthly possessions offer that type of staying power? God will *never* forsake us. How many of our earthly relationships can hold a candle to that?

As we ponder the spectacular display of God's grace in Christ, we fall to our knees in thanksgiving. With the assurance of free and full forgiveness, the security of heaven, and the promise of God's eternal providence, my mantra changes to "It *is* nice." By the grace of God, life is good!

Dear Lord, as I struggle with the temptation of materialism and the love of money, remind me that true peace and contentment are found only in you. Give me contentment every day in knowing that I possess the treasures that nothing can destroy: faith in Jesus my Savior and life eternal in heaven. I pray in Jesus' name. Amen.

Strength from God's Word: What is on your wish list today? What do you need to make your life run more smoothly? Read Philippians 4:12,13. What is the secret to contentment?

ONE HEART, ONE MOUTH

May the God who gives endurance and encouragement give you the same attitude of mind toward each other that Christ Jesus had, so that with one mind and one voice you may glorify the God and Father of our Lord Jesus Christ. (Romans 15:5,6)

Can you imagine the perfect marriage? Take a journey back to the Garden of Eden before the fall into sin. Adam and Eve interacted with each other in a perfect world. Imagine a marriage with no competition, no selfishness, and no tension. Adam and Eve's marriage was a harmonious union in which they had a perfect knowledge of God and a perfect desire to serve each other without any thought of personal gain. And suddenly, BAM! Sin changed that relationship from one of service to one of *self* service. How does that translate in our world today?

Because of sin's entry into the world, our marriages are no longer reflections of the beautiful relationship intended by God but, rather, reflections of our own selfishness. We see the differences that God created between men and women as points of tension rather than as opportunities to celebrate our Creator's wisdom. We become frustrated if our husbands are unable to deal with our emotional breakdowns or when they fail to pick up on the hints we drop them. We belittle our husbands for their inability to match a child's outfit or their belief that frozen waffles alone constitute a healthy dinner. Sadly, these differences become a source of stress and friction instead of humor and appreciation.

In spite of sin's corruption in the husband and wife relationship, God's wisdom is certainly visible in the creation of man and woman. God formed man out of dust and then breathed into his nostrils to give him life and a soul. God created Eve in a different manner, using a rib from Adam, but with no less important purpose in mind. She was to be man's companion and helper. When God instituted marriage in the Garden of Eden, he joined two very special, yet different, creatures to share this lifelong blessing, allowing each to contribute unique gifts to the union of marriage. Husbands and wives have unity of purpose—to glorify God in their lives.

Even though we have knowledge of God's infinite wisdom and purpose, we still allow sin to rear its ugly head in our marriages. Tempers flare, grudges are held, and forgiveness is withheld. How can we achieve unity in our marriages when our husbands allow tackle football in the house and forget to load the dishwasher?

And then there are the things *we* do that irritate our husbands...

On this side of heaven, we will not achieve perfection in our marriages. The devil is prowling around, eager to rob us of joy in our earthly relationships. And he wants to destroy our relationship with Christ. But thank God that through Christ each unkind word and selfish action has been washed clean. The unity we seek can only be found in his Word. Our marriages are strengthened when we spouses take a trip together to the cross of Christ. Clinging to him, we find forgiveness for our own sins and the power to forgive each other.

Go back to our Bible reading, where Paul reminds us how to achieve unity in relationships.

> *May the God who gives endurance and encouragement give you the same attitude of mind toward each other that Christ Jesus had.*

God pours out the endurance and encouragement necessary to run the marathon of motherhood and the strength to put on humility in our relationships with one another.

When my husband and I got married, we chose Romans 15:5,6 as the basis for our wedding sermon. These words are taken from a section where the apostle Paul is teaching strong Christians to bear with the failings of the weak. He teaches us to build one another up instead of tearing one another down. He wants us to glorify God with one heart and one mouth. Isn't that a beautiful picture of marriage? Where one partner is weak, the other's strength builds him or her up. Marriage isn't about who is right and who is wrong. It is about becoming a united front—one heart and mouth—serving God in our marriages and our families. To God be the glory!

Dear Lord, forgive my faults of selfishness, criticism, and unkindness that I show to my husband and others in my family on a daily basis. Help me be a light for Jesus, reflecting his love in my words and actions, both in my marriage and in all other earthly relationships. Strengthen and bless our house so that together we praise the Lord in all things. I pray in Jesus' name. Amen.

Strength from God's Word: Read Romans 14:1–15:13 to learn about dealing with strengths and weaknesses in people. If you have a spouse, each of you should name the strengths and weaknesses you feel that you bring to your marriage. (But you cannot mention your husband's weaknesses; only strengths, and vice versa!) Pray that God give you unity of purpose in your marriage.

SCRIBBLES INTO
A MASTERPIECE

Many are the plans in a person's heart, but it is the LORD's purpose that prevails. (Proverbs 19:21)

My refrigerator is an art gallery flaunting my daughter's artwork to anyone in pursuit of a snack. With determination in her furrowed brow, she spends hours each day creating new masterpieces for the gallery. One day, after a particularly lengthy coloring session, she completed her latest work. Triumphantly setting down the last crayon, she held up her picture and beamed with pride. "Look, Mom, I drew all my friends!"

At first glance, the page was a jumble of red scribbles with no distinction between them. I chuckled, seeing no connection between her red crayon doodles and a group of friends. But as she traced her finger over each friend and explained what she had drawn, I knew the "scribbles" had been carefully planned and meticulously executed. There was sense within the chaos of red on the page.

Does your life ever seem like one giant scribble? The more we attempt to plan the details, the more jumbled up they become. We moms often spend a great deal of time planning things we can't control. The meticulously packed diaper bag is always attached at the hip until it's really needed. Then it's nowhere to be found. The much-anticipated vacation is called off due to an unforeseen illness. Even the plans we make for our children's futures have no guarantees. Most likely, our children will not choose the colleges or spouses of *our* choice.

God reminds us in Proverbs 19:21 that no matter how hard we plan and prepare, God's will is always done. Our best-laid plans are often thrown by the wayside to make room for the plans God has made for us. Yet it is difficult for proud, arrogant sinners to yield to God's will and accept the changes (often blessings) it brings to our lives. Instead we get angry and question God: Lord, why does my child have to be sick now? Why can't we have just a little more money? How could you let me lose my job like that?

Sometimes God's plans for us look like giant scribbles. Things go wrong and are out of our control. We can't seem to make sense of anything. But how amazing it is to know that all things truly are under control! We have the almighty God holding the plan for our lives in his hands. This plan has been carefully formulated and will be meticulously executed by a loving God who seeks only to work out all things for good. The details won't always make sense to our feeble minds, but God truly knows what we need and does what is best. Paul expressed God's promise to us:

We know that in all things God works for the good of those who love him, who have been called according to his purpose. (Romans 8:28)

In spite of the apparent chaos that exists around us, we have the God of order working things out for our good! That is true for our children as well. Although their actions may often disappoint us, God and his Word are at work, molding and shaping their young lives. Although we cannot comprehend God's divine wisdom and power, we do know that the obstacles we encounter serve to draw us closer to him. So when our plans fall apart before our eyes, we yield our sinful minds and submit to God's will. We rejoice that each earthly scribble brings us one step closer to the beautiful masterpiece we will inherit through faith in Jesus: eternal life in heaven.

———————

Dear Lord, although my life may not be going according to my plan right now, I know it is going according to yours. Comfort me with that fact daily. As I fail and my plans seem to blow up in my face, remind me that you are working out *all things* for my eternal good. I pray in Jesus' name. Amen.

Strength from God's Word: Read Matthew 26:36-44. What words of Jesus can you incorporate into your own prayer life? In the reading, how did God use something painful to bring about abundant blessing?

SECURITY BLANKET

Have no fear of sudden disaster or of the ruin that overtakes the wicked, for the LORD will be at your side and will keep your foot from being snared. (Proverbs 3:25,26)

Despite the toy's ragged appearance, my son cannot sleep without his "Baby." Baby has weathered two moves, bouts of the stomach flu, countless nightmares, and every overnight trip my son has ever made. Baby's patched and permanently stained body and his homemade button eyes bear witness to his position as my son's sidekick. I suppose that someday, when my son goes away to college, Baby will find its way into the attic. But for now it provides comfort and familiarity in an unstable world.

As adults, we still seek security in an insecure world. Although we may no longer cling to a blanket or a stuffed animal, we look for security in our padded bank accounts or familiar routines. But if we are realistic about this lost world, we know that no earthly item can give us the security we desperately seek. The daily news, with its footage of earthquakes, hurricanes, and floods, reminds us that nothing is secure. Every day our earthly possessions and even our very lives are threatened by devastation and tragedy. Nothing is secure in this sinful world. Nothing except for the sinless One.

You and I pass through the storms and challenges of this life by holding tight to the one security blanket we will never outgrow—the empty tomb of Christ. We possess the only thing that cannot be taken away from us—the peace and security of having a Savior who died in our place and then rose on the third day. The knowledge that because our Savior lives we too will live stays with us long after the Easter candy has been eaten and the baskets have been put away.

Job, who lost his family, possessions, and even his own health, held on to this security blanket. By faith, Job proclaimed:

I know that my Redeemer lives, and at the last he will stand upon the earth. And after my skin has been thus destroyed, yet in my flesh I shall see God. (Job 19:25,26 ESV)

Centuries later, Peter, an eyewitness of the crucified and risen Savior, echoed the same peace and confidence that Job had:

Praise be to the God and Father of our Lord Jesus Christ! In his great mercy he has given us new birth into a living hope through the resurrection of Jesus Christ from the dead, and into an inheritance that can never perish, spoil or fade. This inheritance is kept in heaven for you. (1 Peter 1:3,4)

25

Often we find ourselves living in the land of fear and what-ifs. The doctor's diagnosis is cancer, the threat of natural disaster circles our homes, or the company downsizes, taking away our jobs. Many things can cause us to waver between faith and doubt. When we seem to have more fear than faith, we need to cling tightly to our security blanket—the empty tomb. It is through Christ's victory that we have victory. It is on the solid rock of Christ that we stand and draw strength to make it through. With confidence like Job and Peter had, we can sing:

> Jesus lives! I know full well
> Nothing me from him shall sever,
> Life nor death nor pow'rs of hell
> Part me now from Christ forever.
> God will be a sure defense;
> This shall be my confidence.
> (*Christian Worship* hymn 145)

Dear Father, I am your dear child. When fears trouble me, keep me focused on your concrete promises that you guide me each day on earth and have prepared life eternal for me in heaven. I pray in my Savior's name. Amen.

Strength from God's Word: Read Luke 2:36-38. What tragedy had Anna experienced? How did Anna deal with the tragedy? Think of a tragedy that you or a loved one has experienced. How can you see God's greatness even in a time like that? What can we learn from Anna about dealing with life's blows?

SILENCE IS GOLDEN

When you pray, go into your room, close the door and pray to your Father, who is unseen. (Matthew 6:6)

Ten preschoolers, driven by the sugar in their Easter candy, did circles in the room. Although outnumbered, I refused to be outsmarted. A serious responsibility lay before me: teaching the resurrection story to these children who had more energy in their little fingers than I had in my entire body. As a last ditch effort to restore order, it was time for a challenge— a game to get their competitive juices flowing. I challenged them to act like the soldiers who fainted at the tomb of Christ on that first Easter morning. The child who could "faint" for the longest would win. In an attempt to outdo one another, the room became silent as the competition began. Ten children lay on their mats with eyes closed and giggles stifled. Eventually each child succumbed to laughter, but now the group was ready to listen to the message. Captivated, the children heard the story of how their Savior earned their salvation by dying on a cross and sealed their eternal life in heaven by rising from the dead. I thanked God for the opportunity to share this beautiful message and marveled at the power of the Holy Spirit at work in these tiny hearts.

How often do we feel like preschoolers on a sugar rush as we race through our daily routines? Some days we are so wound up by our overextended schedules that we don't have a quiet moment until we collapse into bed at night. Other days, when we do have a chance to sit down, the noise from our worried minds drowns out the quiet of the moment.

We know that finding daily quiet time to meditate on God's Word is crucial. It is through this Word that the Holy Spirit comes to us and strengthens us on our walk with Christ. But as mothers, we must admit that quiet time is not easy to come by. Whether it is the crying of a baby, the incessant chatter of a preschooler, or the loud music of a teenager, each phase leaves us longing for silence. We'd love to go behind a closed door, read the Bible, and pray, but sometimes we can't find a door without a runny-nosed kid or a pile of laundry in front of it.

> LORD, do not be far from me. You are my strength; come quickly to help me. (Psalm 22:19)

Have you ever thought of asking God to help you find a silent time to spend with him? It might come in the form of a child's unexpected nap or a spouse's offer to take the kids for a walk. Perhaps you can read a portion of Scripture before your shower, before bed, or in the morning before the rest of the family awakens. You can pray while you load the dishwasher.

In our private time with the Lord and his Word, we go to him for strength and help, first for our spiritual needs, but also for our physical needs. Although finding silent moments may be difficult, it is well worth the effort. Our silent moments in God's Word are awesome. The Holy Spirit is at work. We bow our hearts before the true God and worship him. Silence with God is golden! The laundry can wait.

Dear Lord, be with me today and help me find a quiet moment to ponder your Word. Use that moment of silence to strengthen my faith and trust in you. In Jesus' name, I pray. Amen.

Strength from God's Word: Read Luke 9:10,11 and Matthew 14:23. Why did Jesus often search for a solitary place for himself and his disciples? What obstacles often prevented them from taking those quiet moments? Why do you seek quiet moments in God's Word as well? What blessings await you in these quiet moments?

LASTING GIFTS

Your word, LORD, is eternal; it stands firm in the heavens.
(Psalm 119:89)

There is a photograph of me, suspended in midair with my mouth open, screaming in delight. I had just opened the best Christmas gift ever.

A few months prior to this moment, I had seen the musical *Annie* for the first time. I had come home singing the songs and had my sights set on becoming the next little orphan Annie on stage. I practiced daily for my new role, belting out "Tomorrow" and all the other musical numbers that played from Mom's record album. For months, I ate, slept, and dreamt about my stage debut. It stands to reason that on Christmas Eve, when I opened the box containing a little orphan Annie doll with curly orange hair and a red dress, I was ecstatic.

But the life span of this special gift was short. After only a few months, our cantankerous poodle took a liking to my Annie doll. I can vividly recall walking into my bedroom after school only to find the dog chewing on the head of my favorite possession, yanking out those beautiful orange curls one by one.

Each of us has had a prized possession or a valued gift lost, stolen, or destroyed. Perhaps some of grandmother's china was broken by movers, the diamond from a ring was lost, or a gift from a departed loved one was ruined. We may wish to hold on to such meaningful gifts, but all too often circumstances beyond our control take them from our grasp.

Although we lament the loss of earthly treasures, we rejoice in the treasures that cannot be taken from us. No matter what our bank accounts say, no matter what we keep in safe-deposit boxes, and no matter what is on display in our china cabinets, we possess far greater riches in Jesus Christ. He alone—our greatest treasure—has the power to transform life on earth and guarantee perfect life in heaven. The apostle Paul talks about the amazing riches of Christ Jesus:

Although I am less than the least of all the Lord's people, this grace was given me: to preach to the Gentiles the boundless riches of Christ. (Ephesians 3:8)

We have done nothing to earn our cherished gifts—the riches of Christ. Rather, they are ours by grace alone. Even as we stand safely under the umbrella of God's grace with sins forgiven and eternal life given through faith, we cannot fathom how great these riches are. Right now we see only the tip of the iceberg. We see the love of our Savior displayed in his death for our sins and in his resurrection that assures us of eternal life. We see exactly what God has revealed to us in his Word about our Savior. But so much more awaits us! When we stand by his side in heaven, we will see the fullness of his glory and the treasures that we cannot yet comprehend.

As mothers, we have the privilege of sharing these riches with our children. Because the treasure of Christ has transformed our own lives, we desire to pass on lasting treasure to our children. With the Lord's help, this treasure—our salvation—will be in the forefront of our minds as we share it *day after day* in our homes and beyond.

> *Sing to the LORD a new song; sing to the LORD, all the earth. Sing to the LORD, praise his name; proclaim his salvation day after day. (Psalm 96:1,2)*

As we struggle to provide for the physical needs of our families day after day, let's remember that tending to their spiritual needs is far more important. Every meal we cook cannot stop hunger from showing up a few short hours later, but every nugget of treasure from the Word of God that we feed our children will last into eternity.

> *Jesus declared, "I am the bread of life. Whoever comes to me will never go hungry, and whoever believes in me will never be thirsty." (John 6:35)*

Dear Lord, forgive me for the times I get so caught up in the things of this world that I forget to pass on spiritual truths to my family and those around me. Fill me with the treasure of your Word daily, so that I may pour it out into the lives of others. I pray in Jesus' name. Amen.

Strength from God's Word: Consider the legacy you want to leave. What earthly things do you feel are most important to pass on? Read 1 Peter 1:24,25 and Psalm 119:105-112. How is the spiritual legacy you leave with your child different from an earthly one? Take a moment today to feed your child spiritually by singing a hymn or song, reading a Bible story or devotion, saying a prayer, or, for a child able to read, writing a note to encourage that child's faith in Jesus.

THE FISH SQUISHER

He will cover you with his feathers, and under his wings you will find refuge; his faithfulness will be your shield and rampart. (Psalm 91:4)

Every time we pass the pet store, my children want to go in and "just look." Once inside, their desire to *just look* becomes a need to *have* a pet of their own. I finally caved in to their requests, somehow believing that a fish would be a great opportunity to teach them responsibility. Cow Honeybunny, as he was collaboratively named, had fish food treats and a beautiful tank complete with brightly colored rocks and plants.

For several weeks our fish swam naively around his tank, unaware that he was being stalked by a very curious two-year-old. My son had never touched a fish, and doing so became his main objective. He became obsessed with getting his chubby little hands in the tank and giving Cow Honey-bunny a "hug." Cautiously stalking his prey and waiting until my attention was diverted, he moved in for the kill. After plunging his hands into the water and swirling them around until he caught the fish, he "hugged" the fish with such enthusiasm that Cow Honeybunny later went belly-up.

Do we realize that we are being stalked and plotted against on a daily basis, or are we swimming naively through life? Just as my son stalked the fish looking for any and every opportunity to pounce, the devil does the same to every person in the world, first and foremost, Christians. Satan has but one objective—to destroy our faith. Peter warns us with a vivid picture of the devil:

> Be alert and of sober mind. Your enemy the devil prowls around like a roaring lion looking for someone to devour. (1 Peter 5:8)

Yet in spite of Satan's daily assaults on our faith, we don't need to cower in the corner. We trust the protection of our all-powerful God who sent his Son to live, die, and rise to destroy the devil's works. Satan has been swallowed up in defeat! But even though our Savior has won the victory for us, a daily battle rages on. As long as we remain in this sinful flesh on this sinful earth, the devil will never stop stalking us, trying to choke our faith and drag us away from Christ.

When we feel squeezed by daily temptations, we look to the words of Scripture for comfort. The reading from Psalm 91 gives us two beautiful pictures. The first picture compares God to an eagle. In nature, the eagle expertly cares for its young. When temperatures soar and the sun becomes too hot for the eaglets in the nest, the eagle parents take turns shading them with their wings. What a beautiful picture of comfort when we are feeling the heat of Satan's temptations! Our Lord protects us and shades us.

The second picture the psalmist paints is a scene from battle. A soldier might use armor, a shield, or another type of protective barrier such as a rampart (wall) to put distance between himself and the enemy, but no earthly defense is perfect. Arrows can penetrate armor, and even the most skilled fighter can be conquered by the enemy. A verse from another psalm reminds us that the only impenetrable defense against Satan is the unfailing defense of the almighty God:

> The angel of the LORD encamps around those who fear him, and he delivers them. (Psalm 34:7)

Whenever we grow weary from Satan's attacks, let's look to God in his Word for strength. There he gives us ammunition—the Holy Spirit and his Word—to fight against temptation. Jesus himself used the Scriptures to fight the devil's temptations and win.

Sometimes we feel alone and hard-pressed on every side as we struggle day in and day out against certain sins that we just can't seem to beat. In these difficult times, fall back on the promises of God. These promises remind us that we have value in God's sight as his redeemed children and that God has everything under control, no matter what the evidence looks like.

> Are not two sparrows sold for a penny? Yet not one of them will fall to the ground outside your Father's care. And

even the very hairs of your head are all numbered. So don't be afraid; you are worth more than many sparrows. (Matthew 10:29-31)

Be strong in the Lord. He's got your back. He will protect you from the faith squisher!

Dear Jesus, you fought the devil for me and won. Thank you! Teach me to use your Word to fight Satan and his temptations. Send the Holy Spirit to strengthen me and help me turn from sin. I pray in your name. Amen.

Strength from God's Word: Read Psalm 118. Note especially verse 6. What assaults is Satan waging against you? What is your defense? Review the account of the temptations of Jesus (Matthew 4:1-11). Find Scripture passages to use against Satan and his temptations.

THE GONE 'TUMP

The law from your mouth is more precious to me than thousands of pieces of silver and gold. (Psalm 119:72)

My children usually count down days and spend sleepless nights in anticipation of a trip to Grandma and Grandpa's house. Each trip they are spoiled rotten with cookies, toys, and action-packed outings. Before our latest visit, my three-year-old son was most excited about getting to see the "gone 'tump." We had no idea what he was talking about, but his enthusiasm was undaunted. Much to our chagrin, he excitedly repeated this phrase throughout the duration of the 21-hour car ride. Maybe he was referring to a special toy or place he visited in "Be-con-sin" (Wisconsin) on his last visit. What was the "gone 'tump"?

Soon after our arrival at Grandma and Grandpa's house, we heard the clanging of the railroad crossing and the hum of a train in the distance. "A TRAIN!" he yelled and began running down the sidewalk to the end of the street where he had watched trains numerous times before. And there it was—the "gone 'tump"—a hole in the ground where the remains of a tree stump had been. He had sat on that stump with Grandma and Grandpa and watched trains go by. His favorite memory wasn't the toys or exciting day trips, but sitting with two special people watching trains. To my young son, the time he spent with his grandparents was a fond memory and a dear treasure.

What experiences in life do you treasure? What memories do you hold most dear? Maybe it was that cute little phrase your son used to say as a toddler, your daughter's first smile, or the first wobbly steps your little one took toward your open arms. We mothers cling tightly to those special occasions and attempt to preserve the memories by filling scrapbooks with photos and mementos. We never want to forget how it felt to hold our children for the first time, to teach them to ride bicycles, or to watch them walk onstage and accept awards.

Mary, the mother of Jesus, also remembered the special moments of motherhood. What was her reaction after the birth of her firstborn and the miraculous events surrounding it?

Mary treasured up all these things and pondered them in her heart. (Luke 2:19)

Luke wrote a similar phrase in verse 51 when telling about the first trip to the temple made by the 12-year-old Jesus:

His mother treasured all these things in her heart. (Luke 2:51)

In spite of our efforts to make cherished memories last, time continues to race by. Suddenly, our newborn is a child waving goodbye from a bus on the way to school, and the little girl in pigtails wearing a princess dress is a grown woman standing at the altar to marry her prince. One by one, the memories fade, are forgotten, or are replaced by new ones. Although sometimes we may feel nostalgic for the good old days and may lament the quick passing of time, we also can find great comfort in knowing that each day lived on this earth brings us closer to eternal glory.

As we hold precious moments deep within our hearts, we realize there is much more to treasure. Those moments pale in comparison to the spiritual wealth we have in the Word of God—"the law," as it is called in the first reading. Within that treasure lies the priceless story of our Savior who came to this earth to live the perfect life we could not live, who died the cruel death we deserve, and who rose to seal our eternity in heaven. Our faith in the perfect moments and work of our Savior allows us to have peace and contentment as days fly by. We know that through Christ's work, a perfect eternity awaits us.

So go ahead and treasure the special moments of motherhood. But treasure even more the spiritual riches that are far greater, even greater than all the gold and silver in the world. Through Christ we have the only treasure that will not fade or be taken from us.

Do not store up for yourselves treasure on earth, where moths and vermin destroy, and where thieves break in and steal. But store up for yourselves treasures in heaven, where moths and vermin do not destroy, and where thieves do not break in and steal. For where your treasure is, there your heart will be also. (Matthew 6:19-21)

Dear God, grant us grace today to live a life of obedience and service to you in thanksgiving for the treasure you have given us in Christ. Lead us to ponder and appreciate all that your Son has done for us. Amen.

Strength from God's Word: Read Matthew 13:44-46. How did the two people react when they found treasure? What is the treasure the parables speak about? How can we do the same in regard to the treasure we have in God's Word?

A GLIMPSE OF HEAVEN

I am unworthy of all the kindness and faithfulness you have shown your servant. (Genesis 32:10)

It was the end of one of those memorable days that left my heart filled with thanksgiving. We had spent our Fourth of July holiday at a parade and then enjoyed a meal with friends. Although we were tired from the activity and the heat, no Fourth of July could be complete without fireworks. So we trudged off—blankets, snacks, and two exhausted kids in tow—waiting for the sun to set and the fireworks to begin. From the window of our van, God gave us a little fireworks display of his own. It looked as though his divine paintbrush had touched the clouds with hues of purple, pink, and orange as they caught the glow of the setting sun. Silent with awe, we could almost see the gold-paved streets of heaven in the clouds.

The fireworks were the icing on the cake. We ended the day huddled together, watching the fireworks with the unusual event of both children falling asleep without a fight.

Even though our planet is riddled with sin, our amazing God still blesses us with "heavenly" days here on earth. Whether it is a joyful event such as a wedding, the birth of a child, or a majestic display of God's glory in nature, it makes no difference. These moments seem like a foretaste of heaven and make our hearts swell with gratitude. And yet these moments of pure joy do not come because we have lived the right way or because we somehow deserve them. Rather, these heavenly foretastes come from the hand of a gracious God who often showers us unworthy people with blessings beyond measure. But no matter how awesome these earthly experiences can be, they pale in comparison to what God has in store for us in the future.

> *What no eye has seen, what no ear has heard, and what no human mind has conceived—the things God has prepared for those who love him—these are the things God has revealed to us by his Spirit. (1 Corinthians 2:9,10)*

What exactly does God have in store for us? What will heaven be like? The curious minds of our children often stump us with those same queries. Many have imagined, but no one knows for sure what it will be like to live in glory with Jesus. Even though some verses in Scripture give us glimpses—a few pieces of the puzzle—heaven is still largely a mystery. God gives us one puzzle piece through the writings of John in the book of Revelation:

> *Then I saw "a new heaven and a new earth," for the first heaven and the first earth had passed away, and there was no longer any sea." . . . 'He will wipe every tear from their*

> eyes. There will be no more death' or mourning or crying
> or pain, for the old order of things has passed away."
> (Revelation 21:1,4)

Even with that piece of the puzzle in hand, our minds, having experienced sin and its effects, simply cannot grasp the concept of perfection. Yet we need not sit and ponder the mysteries of heaven. Regardless of what it will or won't be like, one fact remains—we will live with our Savior and be free from sin, pain, and suffering for eternity. This fact is firmly based on God's greatest display of earthly power: when his beaten and bloody Son was nailed to a cross to die for the sins and sinners of this world and then when he rose triumphantly from the grave.

Heaven is ours right now. Jesus earned it for us. So we don't need to know all the miniscule details of our eternal home just yet. Right now our true joy comes from knowing that our sins have been wiped away through Jesus and that our future is secure in a place that God is preparing for us. Any joy we experience here in this physical world is just more icing on the cake.

Whether you are experiencing a foretaste of heaven or a little "hell on earth" in your life today, take heart. This sinful world is only temporary. On amazing days when things go smoothly, fall on your knees before your gracious God and thank him for all your earthly blessings. On days that are filled with struggle and grief, again fall on your knees and call to this same almighty God who has promised to work all things out for good.

Heaven is yours now and forever. Rejoice in what God has done for you!

―――――――――

Dear Lord, no matter what earthly circumstances I am experiencing today, give me an attitude of gratitude. May this gratitude stem not only from receiving many earthly blessings but especially from the multitude of spiritual blessings I possess through faith in Jesus. Thank you, Jesus, for all you have done for me. I praise you and pray in your name. Amen.

Strength from God's Word: What was the best day of your life? Try to list all the physical and spiritual blessings that you experienced on that day. Then try to list all the physical and spiritual blessings you are experiencing today. Read Romans 5:1-5. What spiritual blessings did Paul mention in these verses? According to these verses, how can we maintain an attitude of gratitude in our daily lives, even in the face of trials?

I'M TURNING
INTO MY MOTHER!

Remember your leaders, who spoke the word of God to you. Consider the outcome of their way of life and imitate their faith. (Hebrews 13:7)

Without premeditation, the words spilled out of my mouth. Even though I had vowed never to repeat the phrase to my own children, it was too late. In a moment of desperation my mouth blurted out, "Children are to be seen and not heard!" Although mortified by my outburst, this wasn't the first. This incident was just the latest on a long list of times that I have found myself acting just like my mother.

Without meaning to discredit our own mothers, we may have pledged to do certain things differently than they did. After all, we are a different generation, right? We have new scientific research, blogs galore filled with child-rearing tips, and Google at our fingertips, awaiting our every question. Yet for some of us, this prideful "I'm going to do it my way" attitude evaporates as soon as we have children. Instead of worrying about turning into our mothers, we have a deeper appreciation for all they did for us. I now aspire to be half the mother my mom was.

So even if we joke about turning into our mothers, we cannot deny that what we watched our own mothers do over the years has become an integral part of who we are today. An extremely important influence on the life of a child is the same-sex parent. For those of us with Christian mothers, that is a tremendous blessing. During our childhoods, our mothers spoke the Word of God to us and faithfully brought us to church, and now we have the privilege of duplicating this dedication. For some, that first Christian role model was not a parent but a pastor, Sunday school teacher, or trusted Christian friend who first encouraged us with the gospel. Regardless of the source of encouragement, the writer to Hebrews understood the value of having Christian role models. His words encourage us to model our behavior after the Christian people who taught us and to imitate their faith.

It can be truly humbling to think that someday our own children will imitate our behavior. Daily we must face our own deficiencies and failures. We look in the mirror each night and realize that we yelled too quickly, listened too little, and didn't model Christian living well. While the mirror of God's law shows us our sins and failures, the gospel shows us our loving Jesus standing before us, holding out to us total and complete forgiveness for the wrongs we have done. Now instead of worrying about whether or not we are messing up the lives of our children, we can cling to the sweet promises of the gospel. God no longer demands perfection from us. God's Son was perfect in our place. Forgiveness of sins is ours. God now desires only our faithful service, performed by hearts thankful for what Christ has done.

We parents are like chipped pots and imperfect vessels, yet we hold a perfect treasure to pass on to our children. This treasure is Jesus, who gives us full and free forgiveness, peace, and eternal life. This treasure has far more value than any other family heirloom and is one of eternal consequence. Paul reminds us of the weight of our influence on the faith lives of our children in his letter to Timothy.

> I am reminded of your sincere faith, which first lived in your grandmother Lois and in your mother Eunice and, I am persuaded, now lives in you also. (2 Timothy 1:5)

Timothy's Spirit-worked faith was a legacy passed on by the faithful women who came before him and taught him God's Word. We also have the privilege of leaving this legacy for our children.

Although I am immensely appreciative for the time my mother invested in my physical life, I am eternally grateful for the time she invested in my soul. She made sure I was brought up in a Christian home and received a Christian education. Through this education, I learned the facts that help me not only in this world but also for the one to come. So, thanks, Mom! I guess becoming just like you isn't so bad after all.

Dear Lord, thank you for the Christian role models who fed and nourished my faith with your Word over the years.

Thank you for their dedication and influence. Give me strength today and every day to model Jesus' love in my home by my words and actions. In his name, I pray. Amen.

Strength from God's Word: Read I Samuel chapter I. This section of Scripture reminds us that children are gifts from God. What did your parents (or others) do to foster your faith? What practices can you continue or add? If you were not raised in a Christian home, what routines and traditions revolving around God and his Word can you come up with to follow?

CHEWED-UP CRACKERS

All of us have become like one who is unclean, and all our righteous acts are like filthy rags; we all shrivel up like a leaf, and like the wind our sins sweep us away. (Isaiah 64:6)

Motherhood has changed my perception of gross. Before becoming a mother, I would shudder at the lack of hygiene and manners of other people's children. The simple act of wiping the nose of someone else's child would start my gag reflex and send me into a hand-washing frenzy. Now, as a mother, I engage in disgusting behavior daily. Without hesitation, I catch in my hand the chewed-up crackers my son no longer wants to eat and clean up a variety of bodily fluids without a second thought.

The instant a woman gives birth to a child, she is forever changed. The chapter of life that included sleeping late, eating quiet dinners, and having a clean house ends, and a new chapter begins. This new chapter is filled with heartrending, head-hurting challenges, but it also overflows with terrific rewards.

One blessing of motherhood is that it gives us insight into the concept of unconditional love. Although at times we are frustrated, angry, and saddened by our children's sinful behavior, we still love them—even when their actions have deemed them unlovable to others. And no matter how they treat us, we still deeply desire good things for them.

Now consider the unconditional love of our heavenly Father. He saw the disgusting creatures we are and loved us anyway. He didn't just abandon us to dry up and disappear like leaves in the fall or get blown around and swept away by our sins, as Isaiah wrote about in our Bible reading. Instead, God's great love moved him to act on our behalf. He acted by sacrificing his perfect Son on a cross as punishment for the sins we daily commit. As loathsome and undeserving as we are, Jesus' actions on earth spare us from eternal death and bring us eternal life.

> God demonstrates his own love for us in this: While we were still sinners, Christ died for us. (Romans 5:8)

The love we feel for our children may run deep, but it is imperfect. God's love is perfect and unconditional. God's love never gives way to anger and hurtful words in a moment of frustration as ours does. His arms never tire of extending forgiveness as ours so often do. His forgiveness and love have no boundaries. They extend even to our darkest sins that we keep locked deep in our hearts and that we use to torture ourselves with guilt.

Christ's forgiveness is total, complete, and absolutely free. Rejoice! Our Savior loves us even when we are unlovable to others. His love is so great that it desires what is best for us and has the power to bring it about in our lives.

> *As high as the heavens are above the earth, so great is his love for those who fear him; as far as the east is from the west, so far has he removed our transgressions from us. (Psalm 103:11,12)*

Because of this perfect, unconditional love of God, another transformation has taken place. Through the work of the Holy Spirit in our hearts, we are new creations in Christ. We no longer wear tattered and stained clothing but are clad in robes of righteousness earned by Jesus.

> *I delight greatly in the LORD; my soul rejoices in my God. For he has clothed me with garments of salvation and arrayed me in a robe of his righteousness. (Isaiah 61:10)*

We have new identities. Now we are dearly loved daughters of the King, dressed in holiness, empowered in service, and awaiting his return. How about that for self-esteem! We are not defined by what we cannot do or by the failures we have suffered. On days when we fail miserably or feel depressed, may we see ourselves as Christ sees us—as his beautifully clad, deeply loved, and completely forgiven children. No baggage allowed! Stand before the mirror of God's grace today and see that miraculous transformation—from repulsive sinner to beautiful saint adorned in the garments of salvation.

Dear Lord, although my sinful actions are detestable to you, you still love me. In spite of my sin, you sent your Son to save me and make me your own dear child. When the devil tempts me to doubt your love for me or to beat myself up for my failures, help me to see myself as you see me: redeemed, restored, and forgiven! Thank you for your boundless grace! In my Savior's name, I pray. Amen.

Strength from God's Word: Read Psalm 139:13-16. Self-esteem doesn't come from our accomplishments or what size jeans we wear. How does this psalm give you value? Post the first half of verse 14 on a mirror to remind you daily of who you are!

DON'T MAKE ME COME OVER THERE!

You know the grace of our Lord Jesus Christ, that though he was rich, yet for your sake he became poor, so that you through his poverty might become rich. (2 Corinthians 8:9)

Children have the knack of getting into trouble at the most inopportune times. They can play quietly all afternoon until you begin to make dinner. Then, with sticky pizza dough and flour up to your elbows, you hear the tangle of wills becoming a tangle of bodies on the living room floor. As you continue kneading dough, the situation escalates from a quiet disturbance to a full-fledged war. From the kitchen you threaten, "Don't make me come in there, or you'll be sorry!" But to no avail. Only a parent in close proximity could break up the wrestling ruffians and send them to their bedrooms. There is no such thing as distance parenting.

God our Father, who is never distant, looked down from heaven to see more than a simple disagreement. He saw us wallowing in spiritual blindness with our course set for eternal death. No action of our own could alter this outcome. Yet our heavenly Father didn't turn his head away from us, yell empty threats, or punish our disobedience. Instead, he sent his only Son, who gave up his throne in heaven to come to earth and sleep in an animal trough cradle. Jesus traded his crown of eternal glory for a crown of thorns. Looking at Jesus' life, we see poverty and the sacrifice of his very life; looking at ours, we see riches and eternal life through faith in him.

This great exchange never ceases to amaze! For me, Jesus left his perfect home in heaven where he was the center of perpetual praise and had legions of angels at his command. For me, he came to a sinful world where he knew he would be spit on, disowned, and deserted; where he would suffer complete separation from God and die a death intended for the worst of criminals. He gave up all that he had. And look at me—I quickly grumble and long for a warm bed and a mocha latte after just a couple days of roughing it in the woods.

It gives me chills to think of how deeply my Savior loves me!

> *Because of his great love for us, God, who is rich in mercy, made us alive with Christ even when we were dead in transgressions—it is by grace you have been saved. (Ephesians 2:4,5)*

Even though Jesus' work on earth is complete, his presence in our lives is not. He is constantly at hand to help us through times of physical pain, emotional upheaval, and spiritual distress. He doesn't sit far away in heaven, watching us struggle. Rather, he dotes on us each day, correcting us with his discipline, showering us with his blessings, and strengthening us through his Word. Jesus promises:

Surely I am with you always, to the very end of the age. *(Matthew 28:20)*

What peace and power we gain through Christ's presence in our lives! We have the almighty God, who laid the earth's foundation, on call for us. Our God has the power to send lightning bolts on their way, yet he is never too distracted to listen to us. God's presence follows us to our most crowning achievements on earth and to our deepest pits of despair. He will *never* leave us, even when it seems everyone else has. He is by our sides until he escorts us away from this vale of tears to our homes on high. Thank God that he humbled himself to come here for us!

> Abide with me; fast falls the eventide.
> The darkness deepens; Lord, with me abide.
> When other helpers fail and comforts flee,
> Help of the helpless, oh, abide with me!
> *(Christian Worship* hymn 588)

Dear Jesus, I'll never be sorry that you "came over here" to save me. You exchanged your perfect home to enter and then save a sinful world. Thank you for dying to forgive me and for rising to give me new life. Thank you for being with me always. Help me trust and love you always. Amen.

Strength from God's Word: Read God's promises to Jacob in Genesis 28:10-15 and to the Israelites in Deuteronomy 20:1-4. God made these promises to his chosen people. How can we be certain that these promises apply to us as well? (If you aren't sure, read 1 Peter 2:9,10.) What comfort does this give you in your struggles today?

ENDLESS QUESTIONS

"Be still, and know that I am God; I will be exalted among the nations, I will be exalted in the earth." The LORD Almighty is with us; the God of Jacob is our fortress. (Psalm 46:10,11)

My daughter is an expert question asker. Because I am often short on patience with her curiosity, my daily retort is "Can we do this without asking a million questions, please?" One day while stuck in traffic, the sight of a cement truck brought about an unbearable number of questions. After answering at least ten of them in my kind and patient voice, I let out a huge sigh. She sensed my frustration and said, "Okay, Mommy. I won't ask a million questions."

There is a striking parallel between a child's inquisitive mind and our relationship with God. As we experience trouble and stress in our lives, we often become expert question askers: How could you let this happen? Why now, Lord? Why me? We can be relentless and demanding as we interrogate God, imploring him to fix our problems—NOW! God has the perfect answer to our incessant questioning. In Psalm 46:10, God tells us to *be still*—two simple words that have the power to comfort even the most anxiety-ridden question asker among us. *Be still*—two simple words remind us that God has our future in the palm of his almighty hand.

Jesus also used those two words to rebuke the wind and the waves of the Sea of Galilee. He was in a boat with his disciples when a sudden storm arose, a storm that was so severe that his seaworthy disciples feared for their very lives. But Jesus slept. When his frightened disciples awakened him, he called out those two powerful words and calmed the sea. He also rebuked his disciples:

> *Why are you so afraid? Do you still have no faith?* *(Mark 4:40)*

The disciples' faith needed strengthening. Jesus knew the human nature of his disciples. He knew that even after witnessing countless displays of his almighty power, when the storms of life hit, their faith would still be shaken.

We are no more than doubting, scared disciples ourselves. We stand firmly on the rock of faith until the storms of life hit. Then we doubt and question the Lord of lords and the King of kings. We forget the long history of crises that he has guided us through and allow panic to rise in our throats. We develop stress-induced amnesia, forgetting how all-encompassing the power of our God is.

That brings us to the striking *difference* between our questioning and that of a preschooler—the existence of childlike faith. If I had told my daughter that the cement truck was sent by the president of the United States to pave our way to the grocery store, she would have believed me. A child takes what we say at face value and doesn't question it. Adults are often skeptical and demand proof before belief. Skepticism gives way to doubt that is really nothing more than our archnemesis, the devil, whispering in our ears, "Did God really say that he loves you?" With the seeds of doubt that the devil sows, he seeks to tear us from the palm of our Savior's hand. When we doubt, the devil wins. He succeeds in taking our eyes off of the one, the only one, who truly has the power to help us through any catastrophe.

When doubt creeps up our doorstep, we can combat it with the Word of God and its promises. One great doubt-fighting section of Scripture is Mark 9:14-27. The father of a boy tormented by an evil spirit pleaded in desperation to Jesus:

"If you can do anything, take pity on us and help us."

" 'If you can'?" said Jesus. "Everything is possible for one who believes."

Immediately the boy's father exclaimed, "I do believe; help me overcome my unbelief!" (Mark 9:22-24)

Lord, I believe! Help me overcome my unbelief! We can use these words daily to call to Jesus for help when we are tempted. We can cry out loud, "Go, Satan! Jesus is Lord" to tell the devil and doubt to go away from us. Through Christ, we are victors, not victims! God proved his love for us by sending his own Son to die on Calvary. The deal was sealed when Jesus rose triumphantly and defeated death, the devil, and the world on Easter Sunday. Through Christ, this ultimate victory is ours!

When the storms of life hit and the questioning begins, take a moment in God's Word to be still and listen to his beautiful promises. Although these promises don't cure every heartache, they do fill our broken hearts with the hope of a perfect, stormless eternity. We can almost hear God say, "Can we do this without asking a million questions, please? Don't worry! I've got your back."

And then we can say, "Okay, God. I won't ask a million questions."

Dear Lord, forgive me for the times I question your ways and doubt your promises. Through all of life's storms, give me peace and enable me to humbly submit to your will for my life. No matter what the circumstances, no matter how severe the storm, bless me with childlike faith to trust you fully. I pray in Jesus' name. Amen.

Strength from God's Word: Read Matthew 14:22-34. Why did Peter doubt Jesus? Where did Peter go for help? Think of a time in your life when you doubted. How can you combat the devil when he is on the prowl, tempting you to doubt and question God?

FILL'ER UP, PLEASE!

May the God of hope fill you with all joy and peace as you trust in him, so that you may overflow with hope by the power of the Holy Spirit. (Romans 15:13)

It was quickly turning into one of those days. The night before, my daughter had been plagued by multiple nightmares and my son "forgot" to stay in bed until the sun came up. Even the light of a new day and a fresh pot of coffee had done nothing to ease my grumpiness. And now the laundry pile was spilling out of the closet, both kids were whining, and the babysitter had just called to cancel for the evening. The "night out" had been my only hope of sanity and adult conversation for the entire week. I was running on empty—not enough sleep, too much caffeine, and two kids with panache for choosing the worst possible day to mess with me.

We mothers spend a great deal of time running on empty. The household chores, errands, constant disciplining, and 24/7 on-duty schedule threaten to empty us of all love and patience. It makes no difference what contributing factor is making us high on stress and short on patience. Sometimes it seems we have poured out so much of ourselves into the lives of others that we have nothing left to give.

The world tells us to take time for ourselves. Enjoy coffee with a friend, a day at the spa, or some shopping therapy. While these activities may do wonders to boost our energy and overall mental health, the euphoria they create is short-lived. When the activity is over, the battles with children, the worry over finances, and the stress of deadlines remain. We soon find ourselves drained and empty again.

Believers will have a different cure for running on empty. This cure will not eliminate stress. Stress will remain as a by-product of sin until the world ceases to exist. However, this cure is a source of lasting strength in the face of stress and emptiness. We find this unsurpassed cure in the Word of God. In his Word alone, we find true peace and comfort as the story of our Savior unfolds before us. It began after Adam and Eve first sinned in the Garden of Eden and were promised a solution to sin. It was fulfilled when Jesus lived, died, and rose to earn the salvation that we could not. God's Word offers the only cure for empty lives. When sin and trouble empty us, God is there to fill us with his undeserved love and the peace it brings. Remember, Jesus cried out on the cross, "It is finished!" Our salvation is complete, and through faith each of us has been transformed from an empty void into a new creation overflowing with hope.

When circumstances and events make a day painful, God's Word works. When we feel untouchable—racked with guilt so severe that we are plunging into the pits of hopelessness—God's Word works! Why? Because in the Holy Scriptures we find more than mere words, more than a heartwarming story. We find the power of the Holy Spirit at work. The words of God are not just well-intentioned words of an earthly friend saying, "Cheer up!" without any power to change our circumstances. Rather, they are power-backed words from the Lord of all who is working in all things for our eternal good. The Savior says, "Cheer up! I've already solved your biggest problem, and I am continuing to work everything out on your behalf!"

Have you ever watched a young child fill a cup from a pitcher of water? The water fills the cup and then spills over the sides and all over the floor, carpet, furniture, or whatever else he or she is destroying at the time. Notice that Paul talks about being *filled* with joy and peace and *overflowing* with hope. God's spiritual blessings are unending and unlimited. No, that doesn't mean our problems will simply evaporate. But it does mean that a truckload of spiritual blessings are ours for the taking. Through the power of the Holy Spirit, we have inexhaustible peace, hope, love, forgiveness, and joy. Can you even fathom such amazing grace?

> *You make known to me the path of life; you will fill me with joy in your presence, with eternal pleasures at your right hand.*
> *(Psalm 16:11)*

Troublesome circumstances and events will continue to exasperate us. But no matter how drained we may feel physically, God is there with his promise of spiritual rest. His Word is always available to pour into us. Fill 'er up, God!

_____

Dear Lord, when I am weary, fill me up with the promises of your goodness and love so that I can pour love into the lives of my family and others. Thank you for the spiritual riches of peace, joy, forgiveness, hope, and love that you pour out on me daily through my Savior Jesus Christ. I pray in his name. Amen.

Strength from God's Word: Just as exercise often rejuvenates a tired body, so also exercising your faith by getting into the Word of God rejuvenates a weary soul. Make a list of passages that you can keep in the front cover of your Bible to fill you up on a troubled day. Two of my favorites are Isaiah 43:1-5 and I Peter 1:3-9.

THE LITTLE
VOICE OF WISDOM

Trust in the LORD with all your heart and lean not on your own understanding. (Proverbs 3:5)

Sometimes a piece of advice from a parent, friend, or mentor becomes etched in one's memory. The words become little voices of wisdom that replay in our minds and guide us through difficult decisions.

I received such wise words before my first year of teaching. Filled with apprehension because of my inexperience, I visited the teacher I was replacing to pick his brain for tips on how to run a classroom. With my notebook ready, I listened and waited for him to expound every ounce of his knowledge. Instead, he simply said, "If you say you're going to do something, do it." And? I waited for more. But that was it—one brief sentence—no dissertation on classroom management, no step-by-step lesson plan. Although I left feeling empty, his words have always stuck with me and have guided me in many decisions both as a teacher and as a parent.

We may not have a mental file of wise words to help us solve every dilemma, but King Solomon did. His wisdom was unparalleled by anyone in his day or ours. Solomon's broad scope of wisdom included the scientific knowledge of plants and animals as well as the literary genius that guided him to write approximately four thousand songs and proverbs. Solomon's wisdom was best recognized in his ability to administer justice in his kingdom.

> *King Solomon was greater in riches and wisdom than all the other kings of the earth. All the kings of the earth sought audience with Solomon to hear the wisdom God had put in his heart. (2 Chronicles 9:22,23)*

Solomon had not always been wise, nor had he always felt wise. His father, David, had been known for killing a giant with a slingshot, being a military genius, and writing psalms. Solomon felt the apprehension of his own inexperience as he took over the throne from his father. Without a doubt, Solomon had big shoes to fill. He was young, inexperienced, and inept at handling responsibility. That's when God stepped in. He came to Solomon in a vision and told him to ask for anything he wanted. Solomon could have chosen military success, wealth, or a long life. Instead, he asked for a discerning heart. Solomon wanted the wisdom to rule the kingdom that his father had established. Solomon knew he couldn't do it alone.

God gave Solomon a vast knowledge of earthly subjects, but his wisdom was set apart from the wisdom of the world. His wisdom was centered on the fear of the Lord, the mastermind of all creation. At the root of Solomon's wisdom was the knowledge of the coming Savior who would bring the light of salvation and true wisdom.

Do you ever feel overwhelmed by responsibility and short on wisdom? Being parents gives us that feeling on a daily basis. We have no idea how to handle the never-ending tantrums, the teenage angst, or the pesky rash that doesn't seem to clear up. We devour child-rearing manuals, bombard our pediatricians with questions, and seek the wisdom of parenting experts. But a greater source of wisdom lies before us. Through God's Word we have true wisdom in knowing that Christ died to bring us life. The Bible sets the standards for Christian living that we pass on to our children. Even more important is the sweet gospel message that Jesus Christ kept those standards perfectly and died in our place. In Christ we have the light of salvation and a solid pillar of strength and wisdom to lean on in times of trouble.

Solomon told us to trust in the Lord and not lean on our own understanding. On days when we feel like throwing up our hands in frustration, our wisdom isn't enough to sustain us. But God's wisdom is. The eternal God, the Creator of the universe, gives us the wisdom to deal with any bump in the road.

So while the world seeks wisdom from scholars and from within, our wisdom comes from on high. Although our walk through this life will be tainted by sinfulness and wrong decisions, we still possess the only wisdom that will last into eternity. And this wisdom is not just for us but for our children as well. Through faith created by the Holy Spirit, even the tiniest baby is wise for salvation.

From infancy you have known the Holy Scriptures, which are able to make you wise for salvation through faith in Christ Jesus. (2 Timothy 3:15)

Grow in godly wisdom daily and pass it on! May the loving Savior's promises be engraved in your heart and mind and be replayed daily to sustain you.

Dear Lord, thank you for giving me wisdom from on high that surpasses all earthly wisdom. You have made me wise for salvation through faith in Christ Jesus. Grow this wisdom daily as I study your Word and ponder your promises. In Jesus' name, I pray. Amen.

Strength from God's Word: Read I Kings II:I-I3. What happened to Solomon's faith life? What caused this to occur? What things in your life threaten to turn you away from serving the Lord with all your heart? In spite of the temptations of the unbelieving world around us, how can we avoid turning away from God? (Read Matthew 7:24.)

GIFTS FROM ABOVE

Rejoice always, pray continually, give thanks in all circumstances; for this is God's will for you in Christ Jesus.
(1 Thessalonians 5:16-18)

The same gift can elicit a wide variety of responses from those who receive it. A woman in love with her boyfriend will react differently to an engagement ring than will a woman who isn't sure about her feelings. A child who has experienced severe hunger will react differently to being offered a piece of fruit than a child who has no idea what it means to be in need.

Think back to a similar example from Scripture. The hungry Israelite nation wandering in the desert responded differently to God's gift of manna and quail on day one than it did on day 14,001. God's miraculous provision—nourishing bread and meat from heaven—was met with wonder and thanksgiving at first. But after eating the same food for years, the Israelites grumbled and complained about God's gifts. Clearly, circumstances surrounding the giving of a gift influence how it is received.

It is no different in our lives. When we parents met our new-borns for the first time, we were overcome with gratitude and joy. But enthusiasm and thankfulness tend to dim as we face the grueling task of actually caring for our tiny infants. We tire of the middle of the night feedings, the diaper changes, and the fussy times. This weariness doesn't change as our children age. We tire of making peanut butter sandwiches with the crusts cut off just right, doing mountains of laundry that never end, and waging the same battles with teenagers day in and day out. The circumstances in our lives have a way of derailing us from receiving our blessings with thankful hearts. In the midst of these frustrations, we often don't view our children as blessings, but as aggravations. We face the job of caring for them with resentment. We become like the Israelites who grumbled and complained about God's gifts.

It serves us well to take a moment during these times of frustration and weariness to see what Scripture tells us about the blessing of children. Solomon reminds us:

> *Children are a heritage from the LORD, offspring a reward from him. (Psalm 127:3)*

Years later, Jesus, by his words and actions, taught us the value of the young souls entrusted to our care. At the height of his public ministry, he took time away from teaching and healing to bless little children, even when his disciples tried to brush them off.

> *Jesus said, "Let the little children come to me, and do not hinder them, for the kingdom of heaven belongs to such as these." When*

he had placed his hands on them, he went on from there.
(Matthew 19:14,15)

We cannot help but realize how many times we have grumbled about our children instead of thanking God for them. And how many times have we have brushed off a child's or a spouse's needs to serve ourselves? All too often we take for granted the rain shower of grace in which we stand. Because of that grace and the gift of faith, we journey to the cross for help. There we fall on our knees in repentance, humbled by the magnitude of God's love and forgiveness.

We don't deserve God's goodness. By grace alone, God has given us the physical blessing of family. More important, through faith in Christ, God has made us part of his spiritual family. By Jesus' blood, we are washed clean from every sin and are children of God. And because of Jesus' resurrection, we are heirs of eternal life. This knowledge renews us and motivates us to live a life of gratitude, no matter what the circumstances. True thankfulness comes only at the foot of the cross, rooted in Christ alone.

So then, just as you received Christ Jesus as Lord, continue to live your lives in him, rooted and built up in him, strengthened in the faith as you were taught, and overflowing with thankfulness. (Colossians 2:6,7)

———————

Dear Lord, give me a heart that is content and filled with thanksgiving, regardless of the hardships I may be experiencing today. Remind me that in every trouble, I have all things through Christ. I pray in Jesus' name. Amen.

Strength from God's Word: Read Colossians 3:15-17. Make a list of things to be thankful for today. Take a special look at the circumstances in your life that the world might consider a reason to complain, worry, or be sad. Focus on giving thanks for these trials. Read 2 Corinthians 6:4-10. Why was Paul able to give thanks in spite of the hardships he faced? Why can you do the same?

GROWING UP
BIG AND STRONG

Grow in the grace and knowledge of our Lord and Savior Jesus Christ. To him be glory both now and forever!
(2 Peter 3:18)

Vegetables. I have diced them microscopically, drowned them in dip, and secretly hidden their pureed form in other foods. I have coaxed, threatened, bargained, and engaged in outright deception, all in a futile effort to coerce my son to eat vegetables. Five to seven servings of fruits and vegetables per day become a huge deal for a toddler who will only eat peanut butter toast and noodles. And yet, because of my motherly wish to see him "grow up big and strong," each day the battle begins anew.

Mothers never find a shortage of ways to worry about their children's physical and mental growth and development. We lament over their poor eating habits, sleep patterns, and unkind interactions with other children. We worry, we pray, and we consult other parents. We bemoan our apparent failures, and we celebrate our successes. And just when it seems that one crisis has been averted, another arises in its place.

Yet a far more pressing issue presents itself for our concern. As much as we fret about whether our children will "grow up big and strong" mentally and physically, our most urgent desire is that they "grow up big and strong" spiritually. What can we as parents do to help our children "grow up big and strong" in the Lord?

Although this may seem like an overwhelming task, be encouraged. You are not alone. The Holy Spirit began this work on the day of your child's baptism (and likely earlier, when your unborn child heard you speak or sing God's Word). This all-powerful Holy Spirit came to your tiny baby through water and the Word, worked saving faith, and changed that sinful heart into one that is forgiven and washed clean. God alone can work such a miracle!

> *I will give you a new heart and put a new spirit in you; I will remove from you your heart of stone and give you a heart of flesh. (Ezekiel 36:26)*

This transformation is so simple, yet so complete—sinner to saint; enemy to dear child.

But Baptism is just the beginning of a journey, a journey of spiritual growth that we take every day with our children through home devotions and abundant worship opportunities. And we are not alone in our efforts. We draw strength from the very words of Jesus:

Where two or three gather in my name, there am I with them.
(Matthew 18:20)

As you and I sit on the floor reading the story about baby Jesus, gather family members around the table with a devotion book, bow our heads in prayer at bedtime, or sit in a pew at worship, the Holy Spirit is right there with us. The Holy Spirit plants the seed of faith in Baptism and continues to grow this faith whenever it is watered with the Word of God.

Every day, we can pray for the children entrusted to our care. May the power of the Holy Spirit be with them as they continue their lifelong spiritual journey and "grow up big and strong" in Jesus.

———————

Dear Lord, help my child grow up big and strong physically and mentally, but most important, spiritually, walking in your Word each day. Help me to see each day as an opportunity to teach about you and your mercy and grace. Bless my efforts in this daunting task. In Jesus' name, I pray. Amen.

Strength from God's Word: Read Psalm 34:11. These words evoke a picture of someone gathering children to listen to a story. How do you teach a child to fear the Lord? What are you currently doing to foster spiritual growth? How can you implement more spiritual growth time in your house?

HE CARRIES US

Listen to me, you descendants of Jacob, all the remnant of the people of Israel, you whom I have upheld since your birth, and have carried since you were born. Even to your old age and gray hairs I am he, I am he who will sustain you. I have made you and I will carry you; I will sustain you and I will rescue you. (Isaiah 46:3,4)

Before going on our latest daily walk, my three-year-old daughter decided to exert her growing independence by adamantly refusing the stroller. "I can walk all by myself," she protested. Predictably, my two-year-old son had the exact same reaction. So off we went, exploring every possible inch of the neighborhood on foot. First we discovered some dandelions that would require water and a vase from our house. Then we encountered a rock garden filled with "treasure." Finally, with her pockets filled with rocks, her small hands clutching dandelion bouquets, and her mind realizing she was far from home, my daughter complained that her new shoes were bothering her. "I need you to carry me, Mommy," she said. And, as expected, my two-year-old chimed in, "Me too, Mommy." So our leisurely neighborhood stroll turned into a rigorous workout for me as I lugged both children and their treasures back home in the hot sun.

Christian lives can often parallel such a walk. As we journey through life, we seem to collect more and more responsibilities and commitments. And then the sinful nature exerts an "I can do it all by myself" attitude. So with overbooked calendars and hearts bogged down by the daily frustrations and pains of life, we strain forward. This routine can leave us tired and feeling a long way from home, with hands and hearts stuffed to the max. But because of God's undeserved love, we have someone who carries us when we no longer can walk on our own. Reread the beautiful words of Isaiah. Our almighty God has held us in the palm of his hand since even before our births and continues carrying us into old age. When life is more than we can bear, God is with us and offers us rest from the weariness of this sinful life.

During a conversation with a Christian friend, I was reminded of the absolutely wonderful blessing we have in God's promise to carry us. As a captain in the US Army with two young children, my friend was trying to prepare herself mentally for a 12-month deployment to Iraq. While possessing a brave willingness to give her life for her country, she also had a heavy heart. She was uncertain of what the future would bring for her and wondered how her children would react during her absence. And yet, in the midst of all this uncertainty, she was focused not on *her* strength but on the strength of her almighty God. She knew that no matter what, God would be with her. She was convinced, in no uncertain terms, that when life became too difficult, God would be there to carry her along.

What a beautiful picture—our Father carrying his tired, weary children. This is not just a picture that gives us a warm, fuzzy feeling inside. This is reality. Just as with all of God's promises, when he speaks, he acts. When he promises, he fulfills. God promised the people of Israel physical rescue from the crushing hand of slavery, and he delivered them.

> *He remembered his holy promise given to his servant Abraham. He brought out his people with rejoicing, his chosen ones with shouts of joy. (Psalm 105:42,43)*

God also promised spiritual rescue to the entire world and fulfilled his promise in Jesus. Jesus is the perfect fulfillment of every Old Testament prophecy about the coming Savior. Jesus is true God and true man, who was born of a virgin, who crushed the devil, and who took the punishment we deserve.

Take God at his word. He has promised to carry us when the terrain of this world is too treacherous, and he will act on that promise. Even though earthly struggles persist, we find rest from our sins as God carries us in the palm of his hand. Now may our cries of "I can do it all by myself" turn to cries of "I need you to carry me, dear God."

Rest assured, he'll do just that.

Dear Lord, thank you for your comforting promise to carry me through the valleys of life. As I walk through this earthly life, hold me fast. Comfort me with your promises, give me rest from the weariness of my sinfulness, and bring me safely into glory to praise your name for eternity. In Jesus' name, I pray. Amen.

Strength from God's Word: Read Mark 14:32-42. Jesus told his disciples that he was full of sorrow, to the point of death. What example did Jesus set before us in this text? Make a list of all the things that are weighing heavily on your heart right now, and give them to God in prayer. How do you think God uses our prayers as one of the ways he carries us through this life?

NO FEAR

The LORD is my light and my salvation—whom shall I fear? The LORD is the stronghold of my life—of whom shall I be afraid? (Psalm 27:1)

I live in a house without window screens, so it is no surprise that a significant number of flies find their way into my home during the summer months. Unfortunately, in the middle of a summer heat wave, my youngest daughter suddenly developed a fly phobia. Before she would sit in her high chair to eat, we had to perform a fly-cleansing ritual. She watched (from a safe distance) as I did a perimeter check with the fly swatter in an effort to de-fly the kitchen. As I walloped the daylights out of the visible culprits, she applauded and squealed, "Icky, Icky" after each lethal swat. But if even one renegade fly escaped and buzzed by as she ate, it ignited a tirade of tears and an immediate loss of appetite.

The development of intense, seemingly irrational fears is nothing new for children. My oldest daughter was deathly afraid of sirens, vacuum cleaners, and dogs. My son awoke screaming from unexplained night terrors. Thankfully, it seems that just as quickly as these fears surface, they go away. In the meantime, we parents use any measure of creativity we have to calm their troubled little hearts. Whether we do a nightly check for monsters under the bed or a daily offensive on the kitchen fly population, our goal is the same. We want to calm and reassure our children. But what assurance can we offer? Can we really promise that we won't let anything bad happen to them?

Children grow up; adults grow older. Fears don't go away; they just change shape: the loved one with an unexplained lump, a spouse working in harm's way every day, or the acute knowledge that we cannot prevent bad things from happening to our children. We are powerless to control our lives. What peace can we possibly offer ourselves and others when situations seem hopeless? We can offer the same peace that our almighty God, who *does* have power over our lives, offers us in his Word. Read two fear-fighter promises from God:

We know that in all things God works for the good of those who love him, who have been called according to his purpose. (Romans 8:28)

God is faithful; he will not let you be tempted beyond what you can bear. But when you are tempted, he will also provide a way out so that you can endure it. (1 Corinthians 10:13)

Sometimes, in spite of knowing those two promises, we lie awake at night overwhelmed by anxiety, filled with pain, and afraid to face the future. It is during those heartrending times, unable to stand alone, that we fall on God's greatest fear-fighting promise: heaven is ours through Christ. The pain on earth and storms of daily life are temporary. A calm sea awaits us. Because Jesus died in our place and rose again, we eagerly await our future in heaven. John gives us insight into this glorious future:

> *Then I saw "a new heaven and a new earth," for the first heaven and the first earth had passed away. . . . "They will be his people, and God himself will be with them and be their God. 'He will wipe every tear from their eyes. There will be no more death' or mourning or crying or pain, for the old order of things has passed away." (Revelation 21:1,3,4)*

Now, *that* news is the ultimate fear-fighting ammunition for our adult fears and for our children's fears as well!

I have witnessed people using that ammunition. I remember a family and close friends huddling in a hospital waiting room, their pain-filled faces coming to grips with the doctor's diagnosis: the young daughter-sister-friend would soon die. And yet even in the midst of terrible tragedy, they were not without hope. This group was made up of Christians. Might they have been afraid of the pain of separation they would feel every day for the rest of their earthly lives? Yes. Afraid of the future of their loved one's soul? Certainly not! Grief-stricken, they gathered in prayer, knowing that this girl was about to be ushered into the greatest feast ever prepared. She was embarking on a reunion with her loving Savior and would await another reunion with her earthly family and friends at her Savior's side in his perfect heaven.

Even in death and the heartache it leaves in its wake, Christians have a place of refuge and rest. They possess a peace that the unbelieving world cannot fathom but desperately needs.

When calamity comes, the wicked are brought down, but even in death the righteous seek refuge in God. (Proverbs 14:32)

Safe refuge. Peace through Jesus indeed.

———————

Dear Lord, when I am afraid, give me courage to trust in you. When I fear the future and the unknown, remind me of your beautiful fear-fighting promises in Jesus. Reassure me that you have my family in the palm of your hand—guiding, protecting, and caring for us always. In my Savior's name, I pray. Amen.

Strength from God's Word: One of life's difficulties is our inability to know what the future will bring. We wait for God's plan for our lives to unfold, but his timing is not the same as ours. Read Jeremiah 29:11. This portion of Scripture is taken from a letter to exiles living in Babylon. What comfort does this offer you?

A LITTLE LAMB
AMONG WOLVES

I am sending you out like sheep among wolves. There-
fore be as shrewd as snakes and as innocent as doves.
(Matthew 10:16)

My daughter bounded up the path to school brimming
with enough confidence and enthusiasm for both of us.
Armed with a bag of supplies, a peanut butter and jelly
sandwich, and her glittering Cinderella backpack, she was
ready to take on the world. I lingered behind, masking my
apprehension with sunglasses that hid the tears already
beginning to form. It was a milestone we will always
remember—the first day of kindergarten. For her, the
door was opening to a new world of friends, learning, and
field trips. For me, there was a hollow pit in my stomach.
You see, Jesus had no place in her new school. Creation
would be replaced by scientific theories; God's law, with
tolerance for all lifestyles and beliefs. Humanism would
creep into every subject and attempt to distort her purpose
for serving others.

I had to face the reality that my daughter would not experience 16 years of God-centered education like the ones I had received. Although I've always been thankful for my Christian education, on that day its intrinsic value was unmistakable. I stood at the classroom door, sunglasses no longer doing justice to the tears rolling down my cheeks, and waved good-bye. I was sending my little lamb into the unbelieving world.

When Matthew, inspired by the Holy Spirit, penned the words in our first Bible reading, he was recalling Christ's instructions to his twelve disciples. Jesus was sending his beloved friends into an unbelieving world that would bitterly oppose them and often wish them physical harm. First, Jesus gave them practical advice on how to deal with adversity. He encouraged his disciples to be sly like snakes—quick to flee danger yet also willing to stand their ground if need be. Jesus also commanded the disciples to be peaceful like doves: never picking fights just to win an argument, but, rather, giving the reason for their hope and doing so with love and respect. Alongside this practical advice, Jesus gave them a very important promise:

> Do not worry about what to say or how to say it. At that time you will be given what to say, for it will not be you speaking, but the Spirit of your Father speaking through you. (Matthew 10:19,20)

Knowing that the Spirit would guide their words provided the disciples with assurance when discouragement and self-doubt set in.

As we send our little lambs out into the unbelieving world, we hold on to the same assurance that was given to the disciples: God will be with them.

The LORD is near to all who call on him, to all who call on him in truth. (Psalm 145:18)

We call on our gracious God and pray for our children daily. We pray that God would continue to be with our little lambs, protecting them and strengthening their faith. We ask God to use our cherished ones as lights to bring the message of Christ's peace and forgiveness to others.

You are the light of the world. A town built on a hill cannot be hidden. Neither do people light a lamp and put it under a bowl. Instead they put it on its stand, and it gives light to everyone in the house. In the same way, let your light shine before others, that they may see your good deeds and glorify your Father in heaven. (Matthew 5:14-16)

As friends and classmates of our children see that they are different, there may be questions: Why can't you come for a sleepover on Saturday night? Why can't you play in the tournament on Sunday morning? Why can't you watch certain TV shows? When a door opens, ask Jesus to let the light of his Word shine through. He can use your family to shine his salvation to others.

I can still see a sun catcher hanging in the window at my grandmother's house. It read: "Let go. Let God." As a child, the meaning was never quite clear to me, and it seemed there should be another word at the end. Let God do what? Now the meaning is clear. You and I want to hold on tight, shielding our children from danger and from the disappointments of living in this sinful world. And yet the time comes when we have to let go. When we do, God is there. As we watch our children grow into adults, may we "Let go. Let God." There is no greater comfort for parents releasing their little lambs into a wolf-filled world. God is taking care of them. And he can even use them as lights to grow his kingdom.

Dear Lord, please protect my child physically and emotionally. Preserve my child's faith, and use it to shine a light to the unbelieving world. Help our entire family stay faithful to you and walk in your ways until you bring us to heaven for eternity. In Jesus' name, I pray. Amen.

Strength from God's Word: Read Matthew 9:35-38, a prologue to Jesus' instructions in today's devotion. Before Jesus sent out the Twelve, they prayed together for workers for the plentiful harvest. Today also the harvest is plentiful. List people you know who don't know Jesus. How can you be light to them? I have a friend whose family chooses a different family each year to share Jesus with. They invite the family for dinner, carpool for sporting events, and through the resulting friendship, share their faith. Can you think of similar ideas for your own life as a worker in the Lord's harvest field?

WELCOME HOME

My Father's house has many rooms; if that were not so, would I have told you that I am going there to prepare a place for you? And if I go and prepare a place for you, I will come back and take you to be with me that you also may be where I am. (John 14:2,3)

The road was flanked with a trail of small American flags leading to a house decorated with balloons and a handmade banner. Over 365 days had been crossed off the calendar. With all the preparations carefully executed, the family members were ready to welcome home their hero returning from war. They anxiously waited for his bus to arrive at the parade field. The band played a fanfare as this family climbed the bleachers and joined others, all armed with posters, flowers, and gifts. The air was charged with emotion. The crowd thundered with applause and screams of excitement as the heroes climbed out of their buses and into formation. When a whistle blew to signify the troops' dismissal, the parade field became a sea of mothers, fathers, children, husbands, wives, and other loved ones rushing forward with tear-stained faces and open arms. Welcome home, heroes!

You and I eagerly anticipate our own welcome home ceremony. It is a homecoming celebration far greater than the most emotionally charged military celebration. This amazing moment will occur when we end our tour of duty with the saints militant still battling on earth and join the ranks of the saints triumphant at our Savior's side in heaven. Unlike a military reunion that lasts only until the next deployment, ours is an eternal reunion between our heavenly Father and his dear children who have been washed clean in the blood of the Lamb. Can you picture it? You and I walk through heaven's gate onto a street of solid gold, right up to our Savior's open, outstretched arms. The angels rejoice and the air explodes with beautiful sounds of hosts of believers praising and worshiping God. And there stands our Savior, holding out the crown of eternal life. He wraps his arms tightly around us and exclaims:

Well done, good and faithful servant! (Matthew 25:21)

Although we fervently yearn for our own welcome home ceremony, we must remain here among the ranks of the church militant for as long as God sees fit. Our mission on earth has not yet ended. Everyday we hole up in the trenches, waging war against the devil, the world, and our own sinful flesh. This battle is not easy. Any battle analyst would look at the evidence and presume that we are losing. Our human weaknesses abound as daily we fall prey to the attacks of Satan. We gossip, put self ahead of others, lack patience with our children, forget to put God first, and lose many other battles even before breakfast. This is not a new struggle, but one waged by every believer since sin entered the world in the Garden of Eden. The apostle Paul was no stranger to daily battles against the sinful flesh. He wrote:

> *I know that good itself does not dwell in me, that is, in my sinful nature. For I have the desire to do what is good, but I cannot carry it out. For I do not do the good I want to do, but the evil I do not want to do—this I keep on doing. (Romans 7:18,19)*

The battles we lose daily will not change the outcome of this war. It is over! Thanks be to God that Jesus won the victory over the devil, sin, and death through his life, death, and resurrection. The empty tomb is proof that our all-powerful Savior has defeated our enemies once and for all. And that victory is ours through faith in him! Jesus comforted his twelve disciples (and us!) with these words:

> *I have told you these things, so that in me you may have peace. In this world you will have trouble. But take heart! I have overcome the world. (John 16:33)*

As soldiers of the cross, let's take Jesus' words to heart. On days when we get bogged down in the daily battles, let's keep our eyes on the victory we have through Jesus.

Close your eyes and imagine. Can you hear the angels? Can you see the smiling faces of the loved ones gone before you, eagerly awaiting your arrival? Can you see your Savior's outstretched arms? I can, and I can't wait!

> The strife is o'er, the battle done;
> Now is the victor's triumph won;
> Now be the song of praise begun. Alleluia!

Death's mightiest pow'rs have done their worst,
And Jesus has his foes dispersed;
Let shouts of praise and joy outburst. Alleluia!

On the third morn he rose again
Glorious in majesty to reign;
Oh, let us swell the joyful strain! Alleluia!

                 (*Christian Worship* hymn 148)

Dear Lord, as I wage war with the devil and his temptations, remind me that victory is mine through Christ Jesus. Forgive me for the many battles I lose. Help me not lose heart in the struggle, but yearn for the day that you will bring me home for eternity. I pray in Jesus' name. Amen.

Strength from God's Word: Recall some of the many battles and trials the apostle Paul faced during his ministry. (Look up 2 Corinthians 11:24-29 for help.) According to 2 Timothy 4:17,18, where did Paul receive his strength when facing hardships? How can this reassure you when you battle Satan?

TO FORGIVE AND FORGET

I will forgive their wickedness and will remember their sins no more. (Jeremiah 31:34)

Believe it or not, bedtime at our house is a magical time. Its mysterious power can make even the most frustrating power struggles of the past day disappear. Unfortunately, the process of getting to this peaceful time is anything but magical. In the last moments before bedtime, I wage the day's last battles with only a shred of remaining patience. My two-year-old daughter adamantly refuses to wear anything but her panda pajamas (which are dirty) and asserts her iron will by insisting that she squeeze out the toothpaste, which ends up all over the counter. My blood pressure surges. I take a deep breath, count to 10, and anxiously await the ceasefire and the magic it brings. First, she cuddles up close to me on the rug as we read her favorite book for the five hundredth time. (Ah, my amnesia is beginning.) Next, she folds her hands in prayer, scrunches her eyes closed, and mumbles along with me in her own language. (A few more of the day's past struggles are disappearing.) On the last stanza of our repertoire of hymns, her voice trails off and her eyelids begin to flutter. As sleep takes hold of her tiny body, my forget-fulness is complete. The full-fledged temper tantrum at the doctor's office and the cotton ball "snowstorm" that left "flurries" throughout the house are but distant memories. I no longer see a riotous two-year-old, but only my dear, sweet daughter. My heart swells with love, and I thank God for the gift of her.

There is a striking parallel between the parental amnesia I described and the forgetfulness of our own heavenly Father. Every day we rebel against God's commands and try to run in our own direction. We disown him; we ignore him. And sometimes our iron will screams no in its demand to have its own way. Our defiance doesn't earn us a mere time-out. Rather, the seriousness of our rebellion earns us eternal damnation in hell. No matter what we do, we are unable to earn God's forgiveness, appease his wrath, or live up to his expectation of perfect obedience. And yet, we receive the Father's love.

> *See what great love the Father has lavished on us, that we should be called children of God! And that is what we are! (1 John 3:1)*

What amazing love! Because his Son lived perfectly in our place and sacrificed his life for our forgiveness, our almighty Father no longer sees us as spoiled, disobedient creatures but as his own dearly loved children. Not only are our acts of rebellion completely *forgiven*, but they are *forgotten*. Read the beautiful assurance God gave his straying Israelites long ago:

I have swept away your offenses like a cloud, your sins like the morning mist. Return to me, for I have redeemed you. (Isaiah 44:22)

Just as morning fog is no longer visible in the afternoon sun, so God removes our sins and any trace of their memory.

There is a similarity between our unconditional love for our children and our Father's unconditional love for us, yet an important difference remains. Our love for our children, though deep and unconditional, is not perfect. It is tainted by sin and will be until we reach our home in heaven. While we may have forgiven our children's defiance of the past day, we must admit that we haven't always treated them with patience and love. We lose our tempers, yell without thinking, ignore behaviors that should be corrected, and punish too quickly in anger. As our children age, it becomes even more difficult to forgive and forget. Cruel words spoken to us leave a sting of bitterness that seems impossible to heal. But God's love is both unconditional *and* perfect. He never thinks of himself first. He never slaps us in the face with past sins or holds a grudge against us. He is perfect and loves us with a perfect, holy love.

Who is a God like you, who pardons sin and forgives the transgression of the remnant of his inheritance? You do not stay angry forever but delight to show mercy. You will again have compassion on us; you will tread our sins underfoot and hurl all our iniquities into the depths of the sea. (Micah 7:18,19)

As I watch my daughter sleep, I grow more mindful of the power of my Lord's forgiveness—forgiveness so wide and deep and high that it covers the multitude of sins both my daughter and I have committed in the past day. Sins that should earn us eternal death are gone—completely forgiven and forgotten. The peace this forgiveness brings means a magical bedtime hour for both of us, thanks to our Savior— our perfect, "forgetful" Savior.

> Jesus, Savior, wash away
> All that I've done wrong today.
> Make me ever more like you,
> Good and gentle, kind and true.
> (*Christian Worship* hymn 593)

Dear Lord, thank you for your boundless mercy and complete forgiveness. Give me patience and strength to model this unconditional love to those around me every day. In Jesus' name, I pray. Amen.

Strength from God's Word: Read Luke 15:11-24. The parable of the lost son gives us a picture of our heavenly Father's perfect love and forgiveness. Note the father's actions that show he completely forgave his son. Take your sins and the guilt they create to your heavenly Father in prayer today. God releases you from that guilt and gives you the peace of knowing that all your sins have been completely forgiven and forgotten.

THINGS TOO
WONDERFUL FOR ME

*I do not concern myself with great matters or things too
wonderful for me. But I have calmed and quieted myself, I
am like a weaned child with its mother; like a weaned
child I am content. Israel, put your hope in the LORD both
now and forevermore. (Psalm 131:1-3)*

After a nightmare about a bear attack, my son needed all
the facts. "Could a person really be attacked by a bear? How
could it happen? How could it be prevented?" In an attempt
to quell his fears, we began searching animal books for infor-
mation. But even with some newly acquired knowledge, his
fears remained. Alongside each newly learned fact, a new fear
surfaced: "How many times would a bear swipe at you if
you played dead? Why would God make bears so that they
could run faster than people?"

That last question finally pointed me in the right direction. (Thanks for the teaching moment, God!) It became
clear that a statistical report about bears would not calm

my son's troubled mind. Rather, he needed a lesson about the wisdom of our Creator. I reminded him that just as God had a master plan when he created us with two eyes and ears but only one nose and mouth, so God also created bears according to his master plan. For reasons unknown to us, our almighty Creator designed bears to run up to 35 miles per hour over short distances. After hearing this, my son's questions stopped and his childlike faith took over. Faith in the Creator's divine plan crushed the fears that mere factual knowledge could not.

All too often our first approach in dealing with fears is to trudge through the valleys of life demanding facts and statistics: Why is this happening to me? How long will this last? How will this crisis turn out? What can I do to overcome this obstacle? We deal with each crisis by attempting to gain control of circumstances that are not ours to control. We question our Lord, doubt him, and quite frankly, try to decipher the plans of an almighty, all-knowing God. We often search for facts and answers instead of simply trusting in the master plan of our Creator.

Think of poor Job. In a few quick swoops, he lost his family, servants, health, and wealth. At first Job was patient, but then questions and doubts surfaced. God came to the rescue and set things straight:

> *Where were you when I laid the earth's foundation? Tell me, if you understand. Who marked off its dimensions? Surely you know! Who stretched a measuring line across it? On what were its footings set, or who laid its cornerstone—while the*

morning stars sang together and all the angels shouted for joy?
(Job 38:4-7)

These words put Job back in his place, and they do the same for us. They lead us to repent for all the times we question a God whose plan is much greater than anything we can imagine. God's words not only bring us to our knees in repentance, but they also keep us there in reverence. Who can stand in a valley gazing at snowcapped peaks and not recognize the power of a God whose ways are much higher and wiser than our ways?

As we fall on our knees in awe of our God who transcends time and space, we pray for humility to put God's will above our own will. This humility brings peace:

I do not concern myself with great matters or things too
wonderful for me. But I have calmed and quieted myself.

When we put all matters in the hands of our Creator and stop worrying about things too wonderful for our finite minds, God stills our soul with quiet peace. This might sound like a simple solution, but it isn't. Humanism in our world touts the merits of mankind: "You can do anything if you remain positive and work hard." Our stubborn sinful nature resents giving up control and taunts, "You don't need God. He doesn't really care about you anyway." As the threads of our lives appear to unravel around us and our sinful natures vie for control of the reins, we kneel and say:

I trust in you, LORD; I say, "You are my God." My times
are in your hands. (Psalm 31:14,15)

Whenever I go grocery shopping with my three-year-old daughter, she likes to help carry the bags. She always seems to know which bag contains the eggs and grabs that one first. I hover as she carries it, chiding her to be careful. Because she often swings the bag haphazardly or crashes it into a wall, I usually take the bag and give her one with less fragile contents. What a similar relationship we sometimes try to have with God! We submit to God but then try to take back the reins when things don't resolve as quickly as we'd like. That is when we need to fall on our knees again—daily, hourly, or as often as it takes. Let's stop concerning ourselves with great matters and things too wonderful for us and instead put them in the capable hands of our almighty God!

———————

Dear Lord, today I give you my worries and surrender my will to you. May your will be done in my life today and always. In Jesus' name, I pray. Amen.

Strength from God's Word: Read Ephesians 3:14-20. Write down two specific ways that these words give comfort as you face life's fears and difficulties. Can you think of a time that God answered your prayers in a way even better than you could have imagined in your life or in the life of someone close to you?

A SIMPLE MISUNDERSTANDING

Salvation is found in no one else, for there is no other name under heaven given to mankind by which we must be saved. (Acts 4:12)

Living in a foreign country provides ample opportunities for misunderstandings. One still makes me laugh.

Our neighbor has a fenced-in area for her rabbits. One day, Frau Mayer put one rabbit in a carrier and walked across the street toward our house. My daughter bounded toward her, anxious to stick her fingers into the cage and pet the rabbit. Frau Mayer speaks no English and speaks to me in German as though I understand every word, which I don't. In the course of our "conversation," I kept hearing her say over and over the German word for "cook." Knowing that rabbit (hasenpfeffer) is a German delicacy, I grew more and more alarmed. Could this kind, sweet woman really kill, skin, and eat a rabbit? Every day for the next week, I peered out my window into Frau Mayer's garden to ascertain the fate of this poor rabbit. But daily I saw her feeding it, talking to it, and holding it like a baby. I thought that was strange behavior for someone who was going to kill her own pet. At the end of the week, I coincidentally learned a new word that clarified our conversation. *Gucken* is the German word meaning "to look at," while *kochen* means "to cook." Their pronunciations are similar. So while I had made my neighbor out to be a rabbit assassin, she had merely brought her pet over for us to look at—a simple misunderstanding.

Unfortunately, because our earthly relationships are corrupted by sin, daily misunderstandings abound, even without a language barrier. We want our friends to take our words in the kindest possible way, yet a word of constructive criticism can build a long-lasting wall of resentment. We want to perform well at our jobs, yet a misunderstood directive can cause an avalanche of problems. Our most important relationships are damaged by hurtful words spoken in anger.

There is one misunderstanding we cannot tolerate. A misunderstanding about the nature and person of Jesus Christ is one of eternal consequences. Who is Jesus Christ? A great prophet? A good example? A crutch for the weak-minded fool? Many so-called Bible experts rely on human wisdom and reason when discussing Jesus Christ and his essence, yet it is only through faith in the inerrant Word of God that the characteristics of Jesus Christ are truly known. The apostle Paul recognized that:

The message of the cross is foolishness to those who are perishing, but to us who are being saved it is the power of God. (1 Corinthians 1:18)

Many people throughout the world misunderstand the work of Christ. Some minimize Jesus' sacrifice on the cross by adding works as a requirement for eternal life. Others say that Jesus is their personal savior, yet believe that perhaps Buddha, Allah, or Jehovah could also deliver salvation. They believe there can be many paths to salvation and that each person must decide what is right for him or her. Still others see Jesus only as a means to an abundant life on earth, believing that if they live a certain way, Jesus will spare them from troubles and bless them with prosperity.

In spite of such misconceptions, there is only one Jesus Christ revealed in the Scriptures. He is both true man and true God, who lived a perfect life, died for the sins of the world, and defeated death with his resurrection. Jesus Christ is the only way to eternal life, and true Christians cling to him by the hand of faith. Through Christ alone we have forgiveness of sins and our names written in the book of life. We confess with Peter:

Lord, to whom shall we go? You have the words of eternal life. We have come to believe and to know that you are the Holy One of God. (John 6:68,69)

Through faith, we believe in the Holy One of God. Yet our sinful nature clings to us every day. It tags along everywhere and tries to minimize the person and importance of

Christ in our daily lives. Hardships cause us to doubt Christ's love. We fail to confront sin in our world, thereby squandering opportunities to heal broken hearts with the gospel. We push Jesus aside in our hectic lives. Yet even in the face of this insurmountable pile of sins, we have great joy! In the shadow of Jesus' cross, we stand as loved children of God, completely forgiven. God's amazing grace has no bounds!

Whenever we see the symbol of a cross, whether hung haphazardly around someone's neck or displayed on a wall, let's never forget its significance. Make no misunderstanding! It's Jesus, Jesus, only Jesus! Only through the cross of Christ are we redeemed, restored, and forgiven. To God be the glory!

Dear Lord, I often want you to give me what I want, instead of what I need, and want my own will to be done instead of yours. In times of doubt, I misunderstand you and what you are doing for me. When faced with the world's view of you, I waver. Forgive me. Thank you for being everything to me. Keep my faith founded on Jesus, the rock of my salvation. In his name, I pray. Amen.

Strength from God's Word: Read about some of God's characteristics in Romans 1:20; I Timothy 1:15-17; and Revelation 1:4-8. Think about why each of these attributes is important to you and your faith.

A WOMAN OF CONTRADICTIONS

I find this law at work: Although I want to do good, evil is right there with me. For in my inner being I delight in God's law; but I see another law at work in me, waging war against the law of my mind and making me a prisoner of the law of sin at work within me. What a wretched man I am! (Romans 7:21-24)

My neighbor, her eyes filling with tears, stood in the doorway. Instead of spending the upcoming school holiday traveling or sleeping late, she would be caring for her father who was dying of leukemia. As my own eyes brimmed with tears of empathy, we stood there in a moment of awkwardness. She was clearly embarrassed that her emotions had surfaced so quickly, and all I could say was, "I'm so sorry." To break the uncomfortable silence, my neighbor mumbled something about needing to get home and turned to go. And just like that, another opportunity was squandered. Another wasted moment in the heap of opportunities I have been given to share the reason for the hope I have in Jesus Christ. And while I know full well the peace of salvation through faith in Jesus and his command to share that peace with others, all too often I struggle to put it into practice. I am a woman of contradictions.

The apostle Peter had a similar problem. Peter, named "Rock" by Christ himself, often found his faith rocked by pride, doubt, and denial. On the night before Jesus was crucified, the contradiction in Peter's faith life clearly showed. Jesus predicted that Peter would deny him three times before the rooster crowed. Peter, arrogant and self-reliant, exclaimed that he would never deny Jesus but, rather, would be willing to die with him.

We can almost hear his bruised ego at odds with his Savior's prediction: "Come on, Jesus, I'm 'the rock,' remember?" Later that same night, in a courtyard buzzing with excitement over Jesus' arrest, Peter denied his Savior three times before the rooster crowed twice.

In our Bible reading, Paul tells of this same struggle that plagues every Christian. As we study examples of contradiction in Scripture, let's never appease our guilty consciences by thinking, "I'm not so bad. Even Peter and Paul failed at times." Rather, let's examine ourselves before God's law and see what we really are—poor, miserable sinners. Let's run out of the courtyard with Peter and cry bitter tears of repentance for our own daily denials of our Savior. Then, at the foot of the cross, with tear-stained faces, let's see the sacrifice Jesus made for each of us. He kept the law that we could not, suffered the torments of hell in our place, and came back to life. He extends to us, through faith, forgiveness and eternal life, gifts we could never achieve on our own.

Whenever guilt overwhelms us, there is hope:

Rend your heart and not your garments. Return to the LORD your God, for he is gracious and compassionate, slow to anger and abounding in love. (Joel 2:13)

The devil would have loved to see Peter drown in a pool of self-loathing and guilt over his denial, but Jesus had other plans. One morning after his resurrection, Jesus assured Peter that he was fully forgiven and reinstated him as an apostle. Three times Jesus questioned Peter's love for him, and three times Peter confessed his love for his Savior, not with boasting and bravado, but in humble submission. Through strength from the Holy Spirit, Peter would no longer be a reed swayed in the breeze but, rather, an important tool in building the kingdom of God.

We are all people of contradiction. At church we loudly proclaim the love of Christ, and then we venture into the sinful world and cave under its pressure to conform. We train our children to obey the commandments and then break them ourselves. Anytime we choose the way of the world or sinful self over Christ, we too deny our Savior. But just as our Savior reinstated Peter, so he reinstates us. Although despair and guilt swirl around us and threaten to pull us down daily, Christ assures us of our complete forgiveness and gives us strength to serve him.

Jesus gave his disciples, flawed and sinful people, the Great Commission—to go and make disciples of all nations. It was not their good works that qualified them as evangelists; it was only the grace of God. The same is true of us. Even as our sins contradict the will of God, we continue to be instruments in building his kingdom. Pray that God's power will be made perfect in our weakness as we seek opportunities to witness for Christ, the rock of our salvation.

———————

Dear Lord, forgive me for the times I have failed to share you with others. Put people in my path who need you, and give me confidence to share the reason for the hope I have in Jesus. Use me, in spite of my sinfulness, to be a bold witness of your love and grace at home and beyond. In Jesus' name, I pray. Amen.

Strength from God's Word: Read Jonah chapters 1–3. Marvel at the power of God to use sinners to serve his divine purpose. How did Jonah rebel against God? How did God use Jonah? Pray for opportunities to serve God and share him with others in your life.

GIFTS OF SERVICE

Now there are varieties of gifts, but the same Spirit; and there are varieties of service, but the same Lord; and there are varieties of activities, but it is the same God who empowers them all in everyone. (1 Corinthians 12:4-6 ESV)

Crunchy potatoes and caramelized (burnt!) cheesecake. Yeah, that's what I was about to serve for dinner. Not by choice, of course. Cooking catastrophes occur regularly in my kitchen. Soon after my husband and I were married, I served our pastor lasagna that was still frozen in the middle. Today I served our circuit pastor a hearty helping of stew with half-cooked, crunchy potatoes. For dessert, I offered him a slice of cheesecake with caramel that had irreparably burned onto the bottom of the pan. Unfortunately, I have to admit that this incident is just the latest in a lengthy list of good intentions gone bad.

We see the same trend in our Christian lives. We try; we fail. We have an idea; it is not well received. We want to help, yet end up hindering. We want to serve, and serve in some great fashion, but we just never seem to measure up. As we fail in our attempts time and time again, it is easy to become disgusted with ourselves and concede defeat. "Why even bother?" we say. We tell ourselves that if only we could serve like so-and-so or had the talent of such-and-such, then we would be more valuable to others. In such moments of self-loathing, we fall into the very trap the devil has set for us. Satan knows that workers in God's kingdom who are paralyzed by failure and filled with self-pity are far less effective than those whose focus remains on Christ.

As we evaluate how to better serve God, it is important to remember who we are.

> *We all, like sheep, have gone astray, each of us has turned to our own way. (Isaiah 53:6)*

As wandering sheep, we can do nothing to please God on our own. No work of service can give us a boost into the upper echelons of heaven or earn us favor in God's sight. But there is hope. The passage goes on:

> *And the LORD has laid on him the iniquity of us all.*

Jesus is the Lamb of God who took our iniquities on himself and endured the punishment we deserve. Through faith in Christ's redeeming work, we no longer stand before God as lost sheep, but as his own dear lambs. It is through God's grace alone that we are enabled to serve, and this grace alone ignites our desire to do so.

Even as the Holy Spirit sets our hearts on fire to serve our Savior, our daily battles with the sinful nature wages on. That sinful nature continually tries to pull our focus away from what Christ has done and back to what *we* do. But the apostle Paul, through divine inspiration, reminds us of what is to be at the very heart of every act of service:

Whether you eat or drink or whatever you do, do it all for the glory of God. (1 Corinthians 10:31)

Our works of service don't have to be colossal achievements in the eyes of the world. Rather, they are anything and everything done out of love for and to the glory of our Savior— including the mundane, monotonous tasks we perform daily. Taxiing our children from one event to the next, cutting up vegetables for dinner, or cleaning crayon marks off a wall are all works of service when they stem from a heart that loves Jesus.

A few years ago I took my children Christmas shopping at a dollar store. Because their behavior toward one another was normally anything but kind, I was touched by their request to buy presents for one another. At home, they disappeared to wrap the gifts and make cards. An ordinary onlooker might have thought the gifts were a jumbled mess of jaggedly cut wrapping paper, bunches of misplaced tape, and tags with misspelled words. But to me, the gifts were beautiful because my children had purchased them by their own free will and prepared them with hearts of love for one another.

Perhaps, to some, our gifts of service look like jumbled up messes of good intentions. But we know that all our actions have been washed clean in the blood of Christ. Now, because our good intentions flow from hearts full of love and thankfulness, they are of value to God. Even when our good intentions fail miserably, God's power is on display, for often his glory and greatness shine brightly through our weakness and inadequacies. In all that we do, in success and failure, in great things and small, and in every seemingly insignificant task, to God be the glory!

Lord, forgive me for the times I have envied the gifts of others, thought highly of myself, or failed to serve when given the opportunity. Help me to see every single mundane task that I perform as an opportunity to bring glory to your name. Let my life reflect your love in all I say and do. In Jesus' name. Amen.

Strength from God's Word: Read Romans 12:3-8. What do these words teach about humility as we serve, our purpose in serving, and the manner in which we serve? What gifts has God given you? What roles in your daily life provide opportunities to serve Jesus and others?

THE BLANKET
IS BIG ENOUGH

*I, even I, am he who blots out your transgressions,
for my own sake, and remembers your sins no more.
(Isaiah 43:25)*

An ice-cold foot jabbed me in the back. A flash of lightning revealed another nighttime walker seeking solace in my bed. While the howling wind and crashing thunder alone may not have disrupted my sleep, the addition of two frightened children and a cowering dog to my bed certainly did. After the storm had passed, I lay awake listening to the gentle rain. Shivering, I clung to the only unused corner of my blanket and contorted my body to fit onto the sliver of mattress that remained unoccupied by flailing arms and legs. Cold and uncomfortable, but too lazy to get up, I became convinced that one blanket is simply not enough for a family of four and a dog.

We parents spend sleepless nights caring for the needs of our children. Whether our exhaustion is fresh or a distant memory of bygone 2 A.M. feedings, we are familiar with the challenges fatigue brings to our daily lives. And although sleepless nights are a common thread for parents, most other people have experienced this phenomenon as well. Insomnia, sickness, pain, worry, and stress are all common causes for sleep deprivation. But sometimes our sleepless nights can have another cause—guilt. We lie awake, uncomfortable, not because we don't have enough mattress space or adequate blankets but because we refuse to let go of guilt from past mistakes. We replay the scenes over and over and torture ourselves for tempers we lost, unkind words we spoke, or pet sins we fell right back into. We beat ourselves up and wish we could take back our wrongs. In such moments of despair and pent-up guilt, the devil is getting his way. He has succeeded in taking our salvation out of the hands of Christ and has deceived us into believing that it is somehow up to us. He steals from us the peace that comes through Christ alone.

King David was no stranger to the pain that past sins can cause. Read about his anguish:

> When I kept silent, my bones wasted away through my groaning all day long. For day and night your hand was heavy on me; my strength was sapped as in the heat of summer. Then I acknowledged my sin to you and did not cover up my iniquity. I said, "I will confess my transgressions to the LORD." And you forgave the guilt of my sin. (Psalm 32:3-5)

David had committed adultery with Bathsheba and then orchestrated the murder of her husband, Uriah. David remained unrepentant of his sins until the prophet Nathan confronted him. Nathan told a story about a selfish, sinful man who satisfied himself at the expense of others. When David voiced his disgust with the man, Nathan told him that *he was the man!* (See 2 Samuel 11,12.)

How often haven't we heard that same accusation in God's law—*we are the sinners!* As we hold our lives up to the standard of God's law, we see in its mirror pitiful, sinful human beings, ultimately unable to please God in any way. But praise be to our Lord and Savior Jesus Christ who not only lived the life of perfection we could not but also defeated the devil and his lies once and for all on the cross. Read Isaiah's refreshing announcement:

> *Though your sins are like scarlet, they shall be as white as snow; though they are red as crimson, they shall be like wool. (Isaiah 1:18)*

Bleach can turn stained items white and clean. Through faith, Christ has removed our sin-stained, tattered garments and covered us with white robes of righteousness—sins removed, completely; covered in righteousness, completely; clean like freshly fallen snow.

Sleepless nights agonizing over previous sins cannot and will not make us clean and right with God. Through Christ alone we are able to bask in complete forgiveness and see heaven's gate open wide.

> *God made him who had no sin to be sin for us, so that in him we might become the righteousness of God. (2 Corinthians 5:21)*

If a guilt trip invades our sleep, we can pray for strength to fight the devil's temptation. The blanket of God's forgiveness is big enough to cover all our sins. But an earthly blanket isn't a perfect picture of this forgiveness. When my daughter tries to hide, she covers herself up in bed. Although she can no longer see me, I can see her. Her giggles and her wriggling form beneath the covers are evidence of her hiding place. God's blanket of forgiveness is far greater than any earthly picture of a blanket.

You forgave the iniquity of your people and covered all their sins. (Psalm 85:2)

Snuggle under God's giant blanket of forgiveness that truly is big enough to cover all sins, is powerful enough to erase all guilt, and brings the peace that goes beyond all understanding. That peace is yours and mine today and every day!

Dear Lord, forgive me for holding on to past sins and torturing myself with guilt. Remind me daily that your grace is sufficient, your forgiveness is complete, and because of Jesus, no sin can separate me from your love. As I rejoice in the peace of forgiveness, help me reach out in love to others who struggle with feelings of guilt and worthlessness. In Jesus' name, I pray. Amen.

Strength from God's Word: Read Revelation 7:9-17. Although we have the rock-solid promise of God's forgiveness and freedom from guilt, often our sins continue to torture us and leave tragic consequences in their wake. What further assurances are we given in this section of Revelation?

INCHES AWAY

Now listen, you who say, "Today or tomorrow we will go to this or that city, spend a year there, carry on business and make money." Why, you do not even know what will happen tomorrow. What is your life? You are a mist that appears for a little while and then vanishes. Instead, you ought to say, "If it is the Lord's will, we will live and do this or that." (James 4:13-15)

The images on television flashed before my eyes uninvited. Local programming had been interrupted to bring coverage of the latest world tragedy. Although I had no desire to witness human suffering, the shock and scale of the catastrophe kept me riveted to the screen. Thousands of people, who just moments earlier had scurried through their daily lives without a thought of their own mortality, were now washed out to sea. Lives, homes, businesses, and personal belongings were lost. My heart ached.

We can't help but empathize with those who suffer tragedy. Sometimes the devastation occurs in a faraway land, so we pray for those affected. Other times, the hand of disaster reaches into our own lives. Suddenly, a loved one dies, an accident causes a debilitating injury, or a natural disaster claims our possessions. At such times we recognize the brevity and fragility of human life. We parents are conscious of the lack of control that we have over our children's lives. Child locks, car seats, and childproof containers help us in the safekeeping of our children, but they cannot always prevent accident and injury. We are always at the brink of death.

Do we throw caution to the wind and live with a here today, gone tomorrow mentality? Certainly not. Our Bible reading says that's how unbelievers live. Those who don't know the certainty of their eternity live for the moment instead of asking God's will to guide their moments. They satisfy the desires of the flesh and accumulate as much as possible. However, the insatiable pursuit of "stuff" leaves emptiness and unhappiness in its wake.

The events of John 9:1-7 show that Christians operate according to a different directive. Jesus and his disciples met a man who had been born blind. Likely his parents had eagerly awaited his birth but later realized that their son would never see a beautiful sunrise or springtime blooms. He would have to depend on the charity of others. The disciples asked Jesus whether the man's sins or his parents' sins had caused the blindness. They wanted to know *why.* Just as we do.

> *"Neither this man nor his parents sinned," said Jesus, "but this happened so that the works of God might be displayed in him." (John 9:3)*

Jesus didn't want his disciples to approach every tragedy with a "why did this happen?" mentality. Instead, he had them focus on his promise that even in the most heart-breaking of tragedies, God's glory and amazing goodness are on display.

Perhaps we've seen God's glory on display in the parents of a young girl killed by a drunk driver. Although heart-broken, they draw strength and peace from Jesus' promise of eternal life and they comfort her friends. Or how about a young woman diagnosed with breast cancer just weeks after her husband leaves for a yearlong overseas deployment? She faces the uncertainty of her upcoming battles, knowing that her Savior has already won the most important battle for her soul. And perhaps you know an elderly man who doesn't dwell on the loneliness he feels, but talks about the time when he will see his wife again at Jesus' side. In situations like these, God's works are on display through the faith lives of such Christians. The glory of Christ—the Light of the world—shines through even the darkest moments of tragedy.

Although our lives are like vanishing mists, we still have important work to do—to shine Jesus' light in the darkness around us. Our purpose in life is to know Jesus, grow in him, and share him with others. But this great purpose is temporary. Soon night will come, either on judgment day or when we die. This last day will be the beginning of our greatest glory. It will usher in the goal of our faith, the salvation of our souls.

People will faint from terror, apprehensive of what is coming on the world, for the heavenly bodies will be shaken. At that time they will see the Son of Man coming in a cloud with power and great glory. When these things begin to take place, stand up and lift up your heads, because your redemption is drawing near. (Luke 21:26-28)

Let's live every day as if we are only inches away from lifting our heads to see the author of our faith and the Savior of our souls for eternity. Come, Lord Jesus! Amen.

Dear Lord, when I fear tragedy or experience it in my life, remind me of your promises. Nothing can take away the crown of life Jesus earned for me. Help me hold fast to this truth in the midst of life's troubles and live each day eagerly anticipating the day you will remove me from this world of sadness forever. I pray in Jesus' name. Amen.

Strength from God's Word: Read Luke 12:16-34. These verses deal with the subject of misplaced priorities. In what ways are we sometimes like the rich fool? In what ways can we store up for ourselves the heavenly treasures mentioned in verse 33?

THE ICICLE

The Lord will rescue me from every evil attack and will bring me safely to his heavenly kingdom. To him be glory for ever and ever. Amen. (2 Timothy 4:18)

"Mommy, look what I have!" my daughter yelled, racing to me after kindergarten. Loaded with enthusiasm, she attempted to fish something out of her pocket. Suddenly, her joyful, beaming face transformed into one of panic.

"I can't find it," she wailed as her eyes brimmed with tears. "It was an icicle! I saved it in my pocket to show you, but I lost it!" I smiled to myself at her youthful innocence and at the realization that this was a science lesson she had yet to learn. The large wet spot on her jacket pocket was evidence of exactly where her icicle had gone.

Human beings, young and old, have attempted to preserve treasures over the centuries. Ancient kings preserved valued possessions in elaborate pyramids with secret tunnels and sealed entrances. White-robed museum workers wearing gloves preserve art. Plastic surgeons attempt to preserve the treasure of youthful beauty. Human nature desires to protect our assets for as long as possible. But grave robbers steal, nations at war plunder and loot, natural disasters destroy, and faces carefully sculpted by plastic surgeons will one day be laid to rest in the earth.

We Christians realize that the most precious treasure lies deep within our hearts. That priceless treasure is faith in Jesus Christ as our Savior from sin, faith created by the Holy Spirit through Word and sacrament. But how do we preserve this faith? How do we nurture and care for it as we face the onslaught of temptations in this sinful world? God inspired John to give this advice:

> Hold on to what you have, so that no one will take your crown. (Revelation 3:11)

But how do we hold on, remain faithful, and finally grab that crown of life? Just as we cannot come to faith on our own, neither can we preserve faith on our own.

> No one can say, "Jesus is Lord," except by the Holy Spirit. (1 Corinthians 12:3)

It isn't up to us. If God created faith through the Holy Spirit and then left us to our own devices, we certainly would be no more successful at preserving it than my daughter was at preserving an icicle in her pocket. Without God's help, the seed of faith planted by the Holy Spirit would fare no differently than the seed that fell on rocky places or among thorns in Jesus' parable of the sower (Matthew 13:1-23). Faith might spring up quickly, but it would just as quickly be choked out by the trouble, persecution, and worries of life. Instead, lasting faith is planted in good soil—an area rich with opportunities to hear the Word of God through which the Holy Spirit nurtures and strengthens.

Often we attempt to pin the growth of faith on ourselves. For example, we become stronger and wiser through hardship but then credit ourselves for a job well done. Even when we walk down the right path and avoid the consequences of disobedience, this is not a reflection of what *we* have done but evidence of what *God* has done. It is through Christ's power alone that we are rescued from hell, that our faith is preserved, and that we are enabled to endure trials and to obey our Lord.

> *I am the vine; you are the branches. If you remain in me and I in you, you will bear much fruit; apart from me you can do nothing. (John 15:5)*

After Jesus completed his work and ascended, he sent power from on high—the Holy Spirit—to strengthen his disciples. That power is ours as well. Every time we hear the Word of God, the Holy Spirit strengthens and nurtures us.

Just pause for a moment and cherish the comfort in that truth. In moments of strength, it is the Lord who is at work within us. To him be the glory! In moments of weakness, when our faith is barely flickering in the midst of trial, our God remains with us and continues to work in us. It is not the strength of faith that matters but, rather, the strength of him on whom our faith is built.

Praise be to the God and Father of our Lord Jesus Christ! In his great mercy he has given us new birth into a living hope through the resurrection of Jesus Christ from the dead, and into an inheritance that can never perish, spoil or fade. This inheritance is kept in heaven for you, who through faith are shielded by God's power until the coming of the salvation that is ready to be revealed in the last time. (1 Peter 1:3-5)

Our Lord not only gave us birth into new hope and life but he also promises to guard and shield us with his power until we join him in heaven for eternity. Protected by God's power—that is one method of preservation that cannot fail!

Dear Lord, thank you for the gift of your Holy Spirit and his work of creating and preserving faith. When I am weak or when life's troubles attempt to choke my faith, build me up with your promise that you are shielding my faith by your almighty power. Be with my family and me daily through your Word, strengthening and preserving our faith until life eternal. I pray in Jesus' name. Amen.

Strength from God's Word: Read Matthew 13:1-23. What opportunities has God provided you with to nurture your faith and the faith of those in your home? How can you invest even more in this priceless treasure in your daily life?

REALIGNED PRIORITIES

Start children off [train children] on the way they should go, and even when they are old they will not turn from it. (Proverbs 22:6)

Still in high gear from a busy day, my husband and I sat down for dinner and dug in while the food was hot. We were engrossed in conversation about the day's events and devoured our food in an attempt to finish eating before our newborn awoke.

"Pay, pay!" our 18-month-old piped in from her high chair.

Since her addition went unnoticed as we ravenously filled our faces, she persisted.

"Pay, pay!" she repeated a little louder.

We stopped eating and looked up. As we surveyed our half-finished plates of food, we noticed that our daughter had not yet touched her food. Realizing that she finally had our attention, she folded her hands and repeated, "Pay, pay!" "Pay" was her way of saying *pray*. Humbled by the fact that our daughter, who hadn't yet seen her second birthday, had just realigned our priorities, we folded our hands and gave thanks to God for our food.

It's easy to lose sight of our number one priority as Christian parents. The verse from Proverbs chapter 22 reminds us of this main objective—to teach our children about their Lord and his ways. Although this may seem like a simple goal to achieve, it is not. Every day Satan attempts to distract and derail us from accomplishing it. A late sports practice can upset family dinnertime and uproot the family devotion along with it. A night caring for a sick child can remove any desire or ability to wake up early for a morning devotion. As soon as we develop a new routine of Bible study, the slightest change in schedule threatens to do away with it once again.

So how do we keep Christ as our first priority in the midst of our crazy, hectic lives? We look to God. As we dig into the Scriptures, we see our failings as Christian parents. We have failed to model Christian living and have often pushed Jesus out of first place in our lives. If left with this realization alone, certainly each of us would lose heart, despair over our recurring failures, and throw in the towel. But praise God that in his Word we find hope! As we continue to search this Word, we see God's love and how he proved the depth of his love. He sent his one and only Son to live the perfect life we could not live and to shed his blood to wash clean every one of our failures and sins. As we stay in the Word, the Holy Spirit nourishes us and empowers us to share Jesus' love with others. Every day God's Word gives us power to continue serving him even when we feel like we have fallen flat on our faces.

The time to train our children to love their Savior is limited. All too soon they begin to push themselves out from under our wings and try to spread their own. The same child who screamed when you closed the door so that you could use the bathroom alone suddenly wants you to drop him off a block away from school. As our children begin to push away, we realize that we have many things to teach them before they're gone. We want them to show kindness to others and to learn the value of hard work and persistence. We want them to be independent and resist the temptation of peer pressure. We want them to marry Christian spouses and provide us with grandchildren to spoil. There are many life lessons to teach, but so little time. How can we fit it all in? First, we teach them about Christ, the priority that sets all other priorities.

> *Christ's love compels us, because we are convinced that one died for all, and therefore all died. And he died for all, that those who live should no longer live for themselves but for him who died for them and was raised again. (2 Corinthians 5:14,15)*

As our children learn about the love of Christ and what he has done for them, this love causes them to realign their priorities. Christ's love compels them to live for him, not for themselves. Christ is their reason for living, their passion in life, and their hope when the storms of life threaten to leave them hopeless. Christ is the filter through which all their future decisions must pass and the one who fills them up when they are empty. So, above all, we want to raise children who love Jesus. We want to see them in heaven someday. Through Jesus alone our children truly have a bright future, no matter what happens on earth. It's a future filled with joy and peace, praising their Savior in heaven for all eternity.

———————

Dear Lord, forgive me for the many times I have allowed the busyness of life to distract me from teaching about you. Be with me each day and empower me to make this my number one priority. Be with my family and me and keep us close to you always. I pray this in Jesus' name. Amen.

Strength from God's Word: Read I Corinthians 15:1-4. Paul preached something of first importance—the gospel—to the Corinthians. Read Psalm 63. Write down ways the psalmist described the Word of God (gospel) as having first importance in his life. In what ways can you give the gospel of Jesus Christ top priority in your life and the life of your child? How does the devil constantly work against this goal?

TODAY, I AM NOT

"Very truly I tell you," Jesus answered, "before Abraham was born, I am!" (John 8:58)

My day began with a dropped mug and hot coffee splattered from one end of the kitchen to the other. It continued with my child's full-fledged temper tantrum in the frozen food aisle that resulted in my publicly conspicuous exit from the store carrying a screaming two-year-old and no groceries. Arriving home after the meltdown, I opened the bill for my daughter's most recent medical expenses that far exceeded my expectations. In true "bad day" form, events continued to spiral downward. Because I misplaced the tiny scrap of paper on which I had scrawled the coach's phone message, I drove my son to the wrong soccer field. Apparently, my memory hadn't served me as well as I thought it would. After this fiasco, I made a beeline for home, determined to head off any further incidents. When I entered the house, I was greeted by a mountain of haphazardly strewn backpacks, jackets, shoes, dirty socks, unopened mail, smelly sports equipment, the overdue library books that I forgot to return again, and piles of sand from the sandbox. As I surveyed the chaos, I tried to stifle the lump in my throat and the tears forming in my eyes. After a deep sigh and fewer than 30 seconds of silence, the cacophony of "Mom, I can't find my . . ." and "Mom, can you take me . . . ?" began again, signaling that the day was far from over. I am definitely not supermom.

The illustrious title of supermom entices us all. We all want to be the mom who balances job, children, household duties, schedules, and volunteer commitments with ease and grace—the mom who always has freshly baked cookies and a spotless house. Our quest for perfection often extends to other aspects of our lives. We want to be the super employee, super employer, super student, or super wife. Yet the harder we strive for perfection, the more visible our flaws become. We think we have it all together, but then, one by one, threads begin to unravel. We experience a failure in the workplace, an unforeseen financial setback, or a problem with a child that we just can't seem to fix. Soon, we become acutely aware of what we are not.

When we look deep within ourselves, we find no shortage of imperfections. We agonize over shortcomings, beat ourselves up for failures, and begin to descend lower and lower into depression, self-loathing, and despair. And that is right where Satan wants us. As we focus on ourselves, we are not looking to the one who has done all things well. As we focus on what *we are not*, we are not focused on *what God is*. Instead of pursuing our focus on self, let's sharpen our focus on God, the great *I AM*.

> *"I am the Alpha and the Omega," says the Lord God,*
> *"who is, and who was, and who is to come, the Almighty."*
> *(Revelation 1:8)*

What we could not do, God has done. Where we fail (sometimes miserably!), he succeeds. He fought the battle against Satan and won it for us! He has always been and always will be, and he continues to work the world's events for the glory of his kingdom. Our worth comes not in what we can or can't do but in what Christ has already done for us. When the consequences of our own sinfulness seem too heavy to bear, we fall back on the promises of God and remember that he is almighty. Nothing is too difficult for God to fix!

So on "those days" that remind us of our failures and cause us to realize that we are far from being supermom or super anything, let us look to the cross of Christ. As we stand there, laying our failures at his feet, we can hear him say three short yet astounding words that change who we are today and what we will become in the future.

It is finished. (John 19:30)

These beautiful words assure us that every failure has been nailed to the cross of Christ and removed completely. In these three words we see our value. Our worth is based not on who we are but on what Christ has made us—dearly loved, redeemed daughters of the King. May that comfort and sustain us on even the worst of days!

Dear Savior, help me leave all my troubles, worries, and feelings of failure at your feet. Use your cross to remind me of my value as your child—loved, redeemed, and forgiven. Give me strength to battle the devil, who wants me to despair. Pour out your Holy Spirit to strengthen me as I meditate on the truth that you indeed did do all things well for me. Amen.

Strength from God's Word: Read Luke 18:9-14. After we look into the mirror of God's law and face our sins, we approach the Lord in prayer, as did the tax collector. We come before our almighty God humbly, unable to look into heaven. As we, broken because of our own iniquities and inadequacies, come before the Lord, what does he graciously give us? See Lamentations 3:22,23 and Psalm 51.

NO PAIN, NO GAIN

Endure hardship as discipline; God is treating you as his children. For what children are not disciplined by their father? (Hebrews 12:7)

On my running route, there are exactly 24 large concrete slabs paving the highest hill and 68 rows of grapes lining the second highest incline. I know this because in moments of agony, as I attempt to suck in enough air to sustain my pace going up, I count them. I count them in order to distract my mind from the splitting pain in my side or the burning in my lungs.

I have a love-hate relationship with running. Although I don't particularly enjoy gasping for breath or the vast amount of Bengay that my knees often require, I run anyway. Once the pain has been endured, I benefit from a surge in my energy level and improved mental clarity. So because running brings about positive results that far outweigh the temporary pain, I continue in my daily quest. No pain, no gain.

The phrase *no pain, no gain* can also be an accurate description of our lives as Christians. Sometimes we seem to coast downhill, exhilarated by blessings and virtually pain free. Other times we seem to wage an uphill battle, in pain and gasping for air. We experience ridicule, opposition, loss, and heartbreak. This anguish can be so excruciating that it threatens to plummet us into the depths of despair and drive us to doubt God's love for us. We wonder how such terrible circumstances can come from the hand of a loving God. But God's promises contradict this line of thinking. He assures us that hardships and problems actually prove how much he loves us. In times of trouble, God is treating us as his own dear children, disciplining us so that we fall to our knees and seek him. He is training us in his own wise way.

No discipline seems pleasant at the time, but painful. Later on, however, it produces a harvest of righteousness and peace for those who have been trained by it. (Hebrews 12:11)

The last portion of my run is the most challenging. Although it contains no hills, this last leg contains a straight-away that seems eternal. As I round a corner and attempt to finish the final mile, I see tiny trees on the horizon that seem less than 2-inches tall. As I head toward them, my progress seems very slow. By now my body is sore and my legs are shaking. I want nothing more than to give up and walk home. If I focus on the line of tiny trees in the distance, the desire to quit intensifies because each step seems to bring me no closer to my goal. Instead, I focus on what I cannot see: the finish line that is just beyond the tree line and around the corner. It's my house, and once I reach it, the euphoria of finishing and a glass of ice-cold water await me. I push on toward the goal.

In our Christian lives, our focal point in times of trial is important. Focusing on what is behind often results in guilt and regret. Focusing on the problem itself or on what lies ahead often lends itself to worry. Instead, just as a runner focuses on the finish line, even if it is not visible, we too focus on a finish line. It is eternal life in heaven, where we will finally take hold of the victory that Christ has already won for us. This victory is ours only through Christ's work of defeating sin, death, and the devil with his innocent life, suffering, death, and glorious resurrection. So as we run the race of life, we don't focus on the problems at hand. Instead we keep our eyes on our heavenly prize and run confidently with the victory already in hand through faith in Jesus.

One thing I do: Forgetting what is behind and straining toward what is ahead, I press on toward the goal to win the prize for which God has called me heavenward in Christ Jesus. (Philippians 3:13,14)

In spite of the pain, we press on. We fight the good fight through the power of the Holy Spirit. We await the day on which all our trouble, hardship, and pain will cease for eternity. God be with us as we run our race to eternal glory!

Dear Lord, forgive me when I look to my own ability and strength to make it through daily life. In all moments, whether joyful or painful, help me always focus on your cross and the prize that awaits me in heaven. As I run my race, be with me, strengthen me, and keep me close to you until you bring me into eternal glory. Amen.

Strength from God's Word: Read John 15:1-8, where Jesus describes Christian lives as branches connected to a vine. Who is the vine? Why is our connection to him essential? What happens to branches that don't bear fruit? Who are those branches? Why do some branches get trimmed? Can you think of a time when God used "trimming" to lead you or a friend to him and his Word for strengthening?

A MOMENT OF GLORY

Then the righteous will shine like the sun in the kingdom of their Father. (Matthew 13:43)

It was a moment I will never forget. It occurred on a kickball field in Milwaukee, Wisconsin, on a cloudy fall day. We fourth graders were ecstatic that the upper graders had finally allowed us to play. We were usually denied access to the kickball field and banished to the jungle gym or the smaller field behind the school. But that day was different. Although we still had to endure an occasional disparaging remark from the upper graders, they let us play kickball against them. Surprisingly, we kept the score close. But then the tide turned. The upper graders had the bases loaded and Patrick, the best eighth-grade player, was up to kick. Our narrow shot at victory seemed to be evaporating fast. When the ball left the pitcher's hand, it had a funny spin as it skidded toward the plate. For whatever reason, Patrick kicked it anyway. As he made contact, the ball continued its peculiar, wobbly roll right toward me. The look on Patrick's face said it all. He knew it wasn't a good kick but was confident that no fourth-grade girl could get him out. A smirk surfaced as he ran toward first base. I scooped up the ball and, without thinking or aiming, threw it. The ball hit Patrick squarely on the thigh. He was unmistakably out, and the inning was over. I felt a wave of satisfaction as his smirk turned into a look of utter shock. My teammates' cheers echoed in my ears, and the story of my amazing play circulated throughout the playground. But by the next recess, my moment of glory was forgotten and replaced by the next great play.

It should be fairly obvious from my clear recollection of this trivial moment that there haven't been too many moments of glory in my lifetime. That's likely the case with many of us. Most of us haven't listened to our nation's anthem after receiving an Olympic gold medal or taken a bow before a standing ovation. Even if we were great athletes, musicians, or actors in high school or college, those moments have faded. As adults, we slip into the monotony of daily life in which moments of glory are few and far between. Yet most of us desire to receive recognition for our accomplishments and appreciation for jobs well done. Unfortunately, we are sometimes bitter when no one seems to notice or appreciate what we do. At such times, we look to God's Word to see how we are to work as Christians.

> *Whatever you do, work at it with all your heart, as working for the Lord, not for human masters, since you know that you will receive an inheritance from the Lord as a reward. It is the Lord Christ you are serving. (Colossians 3:23,24)*

The apostle Paul wrote this message to slaves, but his words apply to all who work in service to others. As we toil at work, at church, or within our own homes, we serve our husbands, bosses, coworkers, friends, and children.

But in our efforts, who among us hasn't become a self-promoter? Maybe we tweaked a story, exaggerated an action, or stepped on a few toes to push ourselves into the limelight. Who among us is not content to work humbly for the Lord but instead craves the applause of others? Unfortunately, we are all guilty. We all have been proud and have promoted ourselves above others. We all have failed to give God the glory and instead wore it as a badge to prove our worth to others. God, in his Word, is clear about what becomes of the earthly glory we so strongly desire.

Death expands its jaws, opening wide its mouth. (Isaiah 5:14)

No matter what earthly glory we achieve, how many riches we accumulate, or how much respect we receive, we are all unworthy sinners and we all will die. But our story doesn't end with this bleak prognosis. Enter Jesus Christ. Our Savior saw our lost condition and our absolute inability to earn God's glory and favor. He took on the shame we deserved, died in our place, and rose again in glory. Because of his shame on the cross, we inherit his glory.

Now if we are children, then we are heirs—heirs of God and co-heirs with Christ, if indeed we share in his sufferings in order that we may also share in his glory. (Romans 8:17)

Whether we are esteemed by our coworkers or rejected, appreciated by our husbands and children or taken for granted, it makes no difference. We will all have our moment of glory when Jesus returns. So for now we work, not for earthly accolades but humbly for the Lord. As we perform the same monotonous tasks day in and day out, let's not yearn for approval on earth. Instead, let's work humbly for the Lord with our eyes focused on the eternal glory we will inherit through faith in Christ.

When Christ, who is your life, appears, then you also will appear with him in glory. (Colossians 3:4)

Dear Lord, forgive me when I am full of pride, working hard in this life for all the wrong reasons. Help me fight the temptation to promote myself over others. Instead, give me a servant's heart, and strengthen me to do all things to your glory, not mine. In Jesus' name, I pray. Amen.

Strength from God's Word: Read about Christ's humility in Philippians 2:3-11 and John 13:1-17. Name more ways that Christ showed humility while living on earth. What assurance does Christ's perfect humility give you? Out of love for Jesus, how can you humbly serve in your home, church, and community?

DETOUR

NOW WHAT, LORD?

I the LORD do not change. (Malachi 3:6)

The waiting is over. After nine months of anticipation, your newborn baby is finally swaddled in your arms. But soon you find yourself exhausted, surrounded by baby gadgets you don't know how to use, filled with insecurity, and overwhelmed by responsibility. Fear creeps in. You can't help but wonder, "Now what, Lord?"

Years of your life have been spent at home, caring for your family. Whatever job qualifications you once possessed have long since expired. Although you wish to rejoin the workforce, you wonder, "Now what, Lord?"

The child you so dearly love is stubbornly walking down the wrong path. You feel utterly helpless, with deep pain in your heart. You can't help but wonder, "Now what, Lord?"

A relationship that you treasured for so long has come to an end. You feel alone, isolated, and depressed. You ask, "Now what, Lord?"

The transitions of life often hurl us into uncharted territory and fill us with doubt as we question our next step.

Whether the change is the arrival of a new baby, a move to a new place, or a promotion at work, we wonder how we will cope. Questions swirl around us. Now what, Lord?

Think about Joshua. After the death of Moses, Joshua inherited an overwhelming responsibility. God called him to lead the vast nation of Israel into the Promised Land, an event the people had presumably anticipated for hundreds of years. Joshua knew firsthand the challenges of the job. He had been an eyewitness to the stubbornness of this nation under Moses. As a spy in the days of Moses, he had seen the size of Canaan's heathen inhabitants, their walled cities, and the strength of their armies. In fact, he had listened to 10 out of 12 spies give a negative report about entering the Promised Land:

> *The people who live there are powerful, and the cities are fortified and very large. . . . We can't attack those people; they are stronger than we are. . . . We seemed like grasshoppers in our own eyes, and we looked the same to them. (Numbers 13:28,31,33)*

Only two spies, Joshua and Caleb, had refused to be intimidated by the physical evidence. They knew that with God on their side, the size of the enemy didn't matter. Their God was almighty—far more powerful than the strongest human opponent.

About 40 years later, in a moment that may have been filled with anxiety and fear, Joshua prepared his people to cross the Jordan River into Canaan. Joshua knew that God was at his side, just as he always had been, giving him encouragement and unbreakable promises.

No one will be able to stand against you all the days of your life. As I was with Moses, so I will be with you; I will never leave you nor forsake you. . . . Have I not commanded you? Be strong and courageous. Do not be afraid; do not be discouraged, for the LORD your God will be with you wherever you go. (Joshua 1:5,9)

As we enter the uncharted territory of our own lives, uncertain and afraid of what the future may hold, God comes to us as well. He comes in his Word with unwavering promises to remind us that we don't need to be afraid.

Peace I leave with you; my peace I give you. I do not give to you as the world gives. Do not let your hearts be troubled and do not be afraid. (John 14:27)

Circumstances change. God and his Word do not. His promise of peace does not. That news is our comfort. We may not defeat every enemy or succeed in every venture. But Christ stood in our corner and defeated death and the devil for us. He remains in our corner and continues to fight for us. When the details of our earthly lives don't fall into place the way we think they should, we know that the details of our eternal future will. We have peace beyond comprehension because, through Jesus, our sins are forgiven and our spot in heaven is secure. No matter what the physical evidence may indicate, our Lord stands beside us every moment of every day. He will not leave us or forsake us.

The LORD is with me; I will not be afraid. What can mere mortals do to me? (Psalm 118:6)

Dear Lord, as I experience change and uncertainty in my life, comfort me with your promises and the fact that you and your love do not change. Remind me today and every day that while my life may be rocked by doubt and insecurity, you are with me. Strengthen my faith and give me the peace that comes in knowing you are working out all things for my eternal good. Your will be done. In Jesus' name, I pray. Amen.

Strength from God's Word: Read 2 Chronicles 32:7,8, where King Hezekiah encouraged his people who were under siege by the Assyrians. What reason did Hezekiah give them to be confident, even in the midst of seemingly insurmountable odds? Read 2 Chronicles 32:1-23 to learn how God displayed his power by miraculously delivering Jerusalem. How has (and does) God put his power on display in your life?

EQUIPPED FOR THE JOURNEY

[The law] is to be with him, and he is to read it all the days of his life so that he may learn to revere the LORD his God and follow carefully all the words of this law and these decrees. (Deuteronomy 17:19)

Lists are my specialty. I have lists of long-term projects, wish lists for our budget, and monthly maintenance lists, to name just a few. My list-making obsession kicks into an even higher gear as we prepare for a vacation. In an effort to prepare for any kind of weather or natural disaster, I make even more lists. Once the lists are completed, I spend countless hours organizing and maximizing every possible inch of packable space in the suitcases and the vehicle. But in spite of my efforts, there is always some important thing that is forgotten. One year, my son's winter jacket was left in the car as we rushed to catch a flight. While a winter jacket may not be an absolute necessity during December in Texas, it is in frigid Wisconsin.

We Christians know that the most important item to pack for our journey on this earth is the Word of God. God's

Word is our road map through life. It never steers us in the wrong direction or fails to get us to our final destination. As we read God's road map, we hear the law and the gospel. The law shows us the path of perfection that God demands, while the gospel assures us of God's forgiveness for the countless times we stray from that path. God uses this road map to show us our sins, assure us of salvation, and give us hope of eternal life. In addition, this road map offers guidance in times of indecision, peace in times of crisis, and purpose to our journey. This purpose is to know Jesus and to share him with others.

Yet it can become increasingly difficult to keep this Word of God in the front seat of our lives. At times we become so overburdened with the demands of daily life that God and his Word are easily pushed away and left at the side of the road. Our faltering faith needs a daily walk in God's Word to sustain us through the rigors of this earthly journey. The Bible reading from Deuteronomy is a command God gave to all the kings whom he would place into power to rule over his people. God wanted his leaders to be in his Word daily. He gave a similar command to the people of Israel:

> These commandments that I give you today are to be on your hearts. Impress them on your children. Talk about them when you sit at home and when you walk along the road, when you lie down and when you get up. Tie them as symbols on your hands and bind them on your foreheads. Write them on the doorframes of your houses and on your gates. (Deuteronomy 6:6-9)

Meditating on God and his Word was not to be a happenstance occasion. Rather, God wanted his people to daily ponder their sinfulness, rejoice in his forgiveness, and pass these truths on to others, especially to their children.

Just like the Israelites, we too are surrounded by a heathen world that places little or no value on the Word of God and its truths. The world considers our road map outdated and tries to convince us to put wealth, earthly status, and tolerance first. But our diverse portfolios can be emptied in a market crash, our colleague's respect can evaporate because of a malicious lie, and the blind eye we turn to sin only serves to dull our own consciences. All we strive for on this earth cannot and will not last. The Word of God—the one thing we do need in our earthly journey—is the only thing that will last into eternity.

The grass withers and the flowers fall, but the word of our God endures forever. (Isaiah 40:8)

Through this Word, the Holy Spirit works and strengthens faith. And through this faith in Christ alone, we are able to take hold of the eternal life that our Savior earned for us on the cross.

As we continue on our journey through this earthly life, let's pack our Bibles first. Having the promises of God with us every day gives us the strength to combat Satan and to endure all the bumps in the road. May God grant each of us safe travels until we meet again in heaven!

Dear Lord, as I journey through this life, help me always keep your Word right beside me. Build me up through my personal study of your Word so that I pass on love for you and your Word to my family. Send the Holy Spirit to strengthen my faith and equip me to handle any bumps in the road. In Jesus' name. Amen.

Strength from God's Word: Read Deuteronomy 8:3. With these words, God reminded the Israelites (and reminds us) that nothing is more important than his Word. We would not willingly go an entire day without eating food. Neither should we go without spiritual food. How can you make eating the Bread of Life daily a priority? Be creative. Look back to Deuteronomy 6:6-9 and think of some ways that you can take God's Word along with your on-the-go lifestyle. Talk to your pastor and Christian friends for ideas and encouragement.